Story Central Reader 5

Contents

Chapter 1

A Boy Named Edward

5
He was in his classroom, but it was different. There wasn't a laptop or whiteboard, there was a chalkboard and chalk. The children used ink pens and big dictionaries. No one saw Zak.
12:45
6
Then a boy said, "Come and sit here." Zak sat down next to the boy. "I'm Edward," said the boy.
7
"We have to write about the Aztecs," said Edward. "I love history."
"Really?" asked Zak.
"Yes," said Edward. He opened his encyclopedia. "Look! Look at the amazing temples the Aztecs built …"
"Oh, that is kind of interesting. I guess I've never thought about that before," said Zak.
At twelve forty-five, the bell rang. "It's lunchtime!" said Edward. "Let's go outside. Do you have a cap? It's cold."

8 Edward ran onto the playground. Zak watched. This was his school. Some boys were playing tag. Some girls were playing with hula-hoops. "Come and play," said Edward.

9 "Who are you talking to, Edward?" laughed another boy. "Your imaginary friend?" The boys chased Edward. He ran away. His cap fell off. Zak wanted to help Edward. He was picking up Edward's cap when the boys ran past and knocked him over.

10
Suddenly, the bell rang. It was the end of lunchtime. Zak was in his own classroom. His head hurt. He had Edward's cap in his hand.
Mr. Cunningham walked in. "So, Zachary Harris," he said. "DON'T use your phone in class again."
11
Then, he saw the cap. "I used to wear a cap like that at school," he said. "EHC: Edward Howard Cunningham! That's me!" said Mr. Cunningham. "I remember this cap. I lost it on this playground almost 60 years ago. Thank you!"
E.H.C
12:45
12
Mr. Cunningham started to walk away. "When I was your age, I had a very good friend. He was named Zak, too."
"Mr. Cunningham," said Zak. "I'm sorry I misbehaved in class. This lunchtime, I learned something about the past. You're right. History *is* interesting."

Chapter 2 Andy and Grant

1

Grant was sunbathing and listening to music when he saw his friend Andy carrying some corn.

"Hey, Andy!" said Grant. "I haven't seen you for ages. Where have you been?"

"We've been in the field," answered Andy.

"What are you doing?" asked Grant. "Why are you working so hard? It's a beautiful day."

"We're collecting corn for the winter. We haven't finished yet," said Andy. "How long have you been there?"

"I've been here for months," said Grant. "I've slept a lot and enjoyed the sun. I wanted to learn how to play chess, but the ants don't want to play with me. So, I've read some poetry, in Japanese! I've done some photography and … hey! I've written a song. Listen. I might learn some karate next!"

2

"Yes, yes, you're very smart," said Andy. "And I'm very busy." He picked up the corn and carried it to a hole in the ground.

"You should relax more," said Grant. "There's plenty of food right now." Grant pulled a leaf from a plant and ate it.

3

"Ants are so stupid," Grant thought. "I've relaxed in the sun every day since the spring. I've never wasted time working in the summer."

"When are you going to stop?" asked Grant.

"We're going to stop in the fall when we've collected all the corn. Ants have lived in this field for many years. We've collected corn all summer, every summer, for hundreds of years. It's what ants do!"

"Haven't you heard? It's going to be a very cold winter," said Andy. But Grant wasn't listening. He was listening to his music and singing his song.

"Goodbye," said Andy. "I'm going to collect some more corn. I might see you later."

4 Summer turned to fall and fall turned to winter. The days were short and gray. The nights were long and dark. Grant was cold and hungry. There was no food. Then, he remembered the ants.

"I haven't seen them for a long time," he thought. "I'm going to find them. They might give me some food."

5 He went to Andy's house. Andy was baking a corn cake. "Hey, Andy! That cake smells good. I'm hungry," he said.

Andy said, "Sorry! I worked hard all summer while you were relaxing and listening to music. You've enjoyed yourself but you haven't been very smart. I can't help you. I need this corn for my family."

And he shut the door in Grant's face.

6 "What have I done? I've been so stupid," said Grant. "I didn't use my time well … and I've lost a friend."

Chapter 3

DOWN THE RABBIT HOLE

3
Now she was sitting in a dark hallway. She saw a little door and behind the door there was the most beautiful garden. On a small table, there was a key.
She wanted to go into the garden but she was too big. Suddenly she noticed a little bottle. On the bottle she read the words "DRINK ME." She opened the bottle and drank.
"What a strange feeling!" said Alice. "I'm getting smaller."
Soon she was very small. Unfortunately, the key was on the table, and she wasn't as tall as the table. She sat down and cried. It was so disappointing.

4
eat me!
Then Alice saw a cake. She read the words, "EAT ME.""Well, I'm going to eat it," said Alice, "and if I grow taller, I can reach the key. If I grow smaller, I can crawl under the door."
She ate a little bit. Nothing happened. So Alice finished the cake.

5
"Stranger and stranger!" cried Alice. "Now I'm growing taller." Fortunately, Alice was really tall now. She picked up the key and opened the door.

6
Poor Alice! She looked into the garden with one eye. Her head was bigger than the door. "How embarrassing," thought Alice. She started to cry again. Soon there was a large pool of tears.
7
Finally the White Rabbit came back, wearing a nice suit. He was carrying gloves and a large fan.
"Please, sir," said Alice. But Alice was big and frightening. The Rabbit dropped his fan, and ran away.
Alice was very hot so she used the fan. "This is confusing. Where am I?" she said. Soon she was cooler, but also smaller! "This is weird," she said. "But now I can go into the garden."
8
But the door was closed and the key was on the table again. "Oh, no! I can't reach the key now," she said. She was too small again. Suddenly she fell into some water. "Am I in the ocean?" she asked. "Oh, these are my tears," she remembered.
9
"Wake up, Alice!" said her sister. "Did you sleep well?"
"Yes, I did," said Alice. "I had the most amazing dream! It was just as realistic as now." She told her sister about her amazing adventures.
"Run inside, it's getting late," said her sister.
Alice got up. "What a wonderful dream!" she thought. Then, she saw a white rabbit running behind a tree.

Chapter 4
THE GREAT BALLOON ADVENTURE
1 Doctor Samuel Ferguson's study.
What are you doing for vacation, Richard?
Oh, nothing much, Samuel. I'm hanging out at home.
OK! You're coming with me! We're going on a trip.
2 Here's the itinerary. We're leaving in the spring! We're taking off from the island of Zanzibar, close to the east coast of Africa. Joe! Have my bags packed and ready then.
3
Flying?
We're flying west over Lake Victoria.
Yes! In a hot air balloon. A balloon flight! Then we're flying to Lake Chad. After that, we're going to Timbuktu and then to the west coast.

4
Can I come too, Doctor?
No, Joe, you're too young. We're looking for adventure! We're going to find the source of the Nile.
5
One month later. Spring time, Zanzibar.
6
Joe! What are you doing here?
I'm sorry! I want to see Africa, too.
Well, I hope the balloon will carry all three passengers.

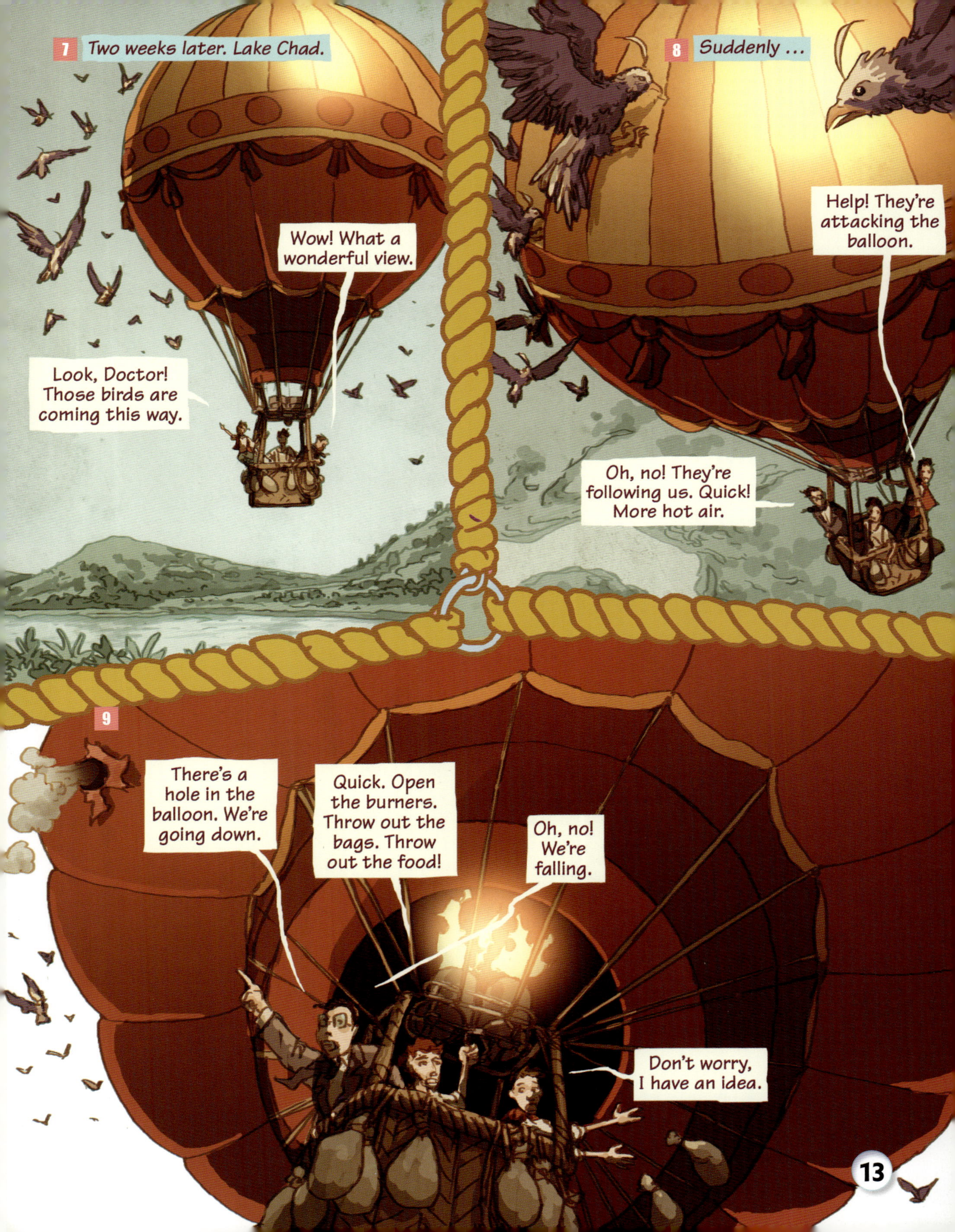
7
Two weeks later. Lake Chad.
Wow! What a wonderful view.
Look, Doctor! Those birds are coming this way.
8
Suddenly …
Help! They're attacking the balloon.
Oh, no! They're following us. Quick! More hot air.
9
There's a hole in the balloon. We're going down.
Quick. Open the burners. Throw out the bags. Throw out the food!
Oh, no! We're falling.
Don't worry, I have an idea.

10
Joe! No!
11
SPLASH
12
Later, close to the lake...
Let's fix the balloon and sleep here tonight. But tomorrow, we're going back to find Joe.
Poor Joe. I hope he's safe.

13
Meanwhile...
I know there are crocodiles in the water, but I have to swim to land.

14

15
I am so tired. I'm going to sleep in this tree.

16
The next morning...
The wind is blowing to the east. We're going back to the lake. He might see the balloon.

17
I can't believe it! It's the balloon. My friends are here.
18
Look! There's Joe.
Smart Joe! He's running in the same direction as the wind. But we're going too fast.

19
We can't land here, Joe! There are too many trees.
Come on, boy, we're going for a ride.
20
Throw him the rope!
Catch it, Joe!
21
Jump in, Joe.

22
Joe, you are safe now.
Thank you.
More hot air, Doctor!
We're going to go home now.
23
A year later...
What are you doing for vacation this year?
Nothing much, I'm staying home... I *am* staying home. I'm *not* going on any more of your adventures.

Chapter 5 THIS STRANGE LAND

1

Let me tell you about my dream,
When I sailed along a lemonade stream,
In a boat made of lettuce and sails made of cheese,
To a land where chocolate grows on trees.

This strange land is ruled by a queen.
She lives in a castle made of ice cream.
The castle tower isn't made of stone,
It's a delicious, yellow ice cream cone.

The queen's crown is made of gold,
Her clothes are soft, white silk, I'm told.
"Welcome!" says the queen to me,
"Help yourself to food. It's free."

The chairs and tables aren't made of wood,
They're made of cookies. They're very good,
Sugar is used for windows, not glass,
The fields are made of green leather, not grass.

2

The queen never smiles. She just looks sad,
Is living here really so bad?
She says to me, "Make yourself at home,
But don't catch the fish when you're alone."

My boat sails slowly through night and day,
Passing mountains and cotton fields along the way,
There are clouds made of wool and trees of bread,
And cute paper birds fly over my head.

3

In the water are small chocolate fish,
They swim around and splash and splish,
"Let's catch a chocolate fish," I think.
I need something now to eat and drink.

I sit in my boat and catch some fish,
They aren't easy to catch, but they're easy to miss,
"I've caught one!" I shout. "Don't let it go!"
But the boat starts to sway to and fro.

4

Where the stream meets the big gray sea,
There is nothing for miles, just the boat and me,
When the wind blows, the boat starts to shake,
When the rain falls, the monsters wake.

5

Then a giant fish made of lemon jell-o,
Jumps out of the water. He's big and yellow!
He opens his mouth to take a bite,
I can see his teeth in the moonlight.

6

He smashes the boat with his big yellow tail,
He eats the lettuce, and the cheese sail,
"Remember, he's made of jell-o," I think,
But then my little boat starts to sink.

7

I pick up a plastic spoon and I give him a poke,
The jell-o fish starts to cough and choke,
"Wake up!" I shout, "It's only a dream!"
Then I eat him for breakfast with
strawberries and cream!

8

My poor little boat is now broken in pieces,
It floats in the water—tasty little lettuces,
Next time I go sailing, maybe I should,
Go in a boat that's made of wood.

Chapter 6

The Journal

① **Amy:** (*waking suddenly with a gasp, then whispering to self*) What was that?
(*calling out*) Aunt Edith! Auntie! Are you OK?

② *Monday, April 15th, 1912*

I was sleeping in bed when a loud noise woke me up. Then a man knocked on my door. He said, "Come to the boat deck and bring your life jacket." I was frightened. While I was putting on my clothes and life jacket, I put this journal into my pocket.

④ *There were a lot of people in the hallway. My aunt was wearing her nightclothes and a coat when she came out of her cabin. No one was running or shouting. Everyone was talking quietly.*

Aunt Edith: It's OK, I'm here, Amy.
Amy: Where are we going? What's happening?
Crew member: We hit an iceberg.
Amy: *(slowly and seriously)* Is the ship sinking? Are we going to drown?
Crew member: No. It's OK. Don't worry. The Titanic is unsinkable! It's the best ship ever built.

⑥ It was cold and dark outside. We were standing on the deck when an enormous iceberg passed us. It looked like a huge, white rock. Pieces of ice were falling off it onto the deck. Some children made snowballs from the ice and threw them into the water. It was warm and light inside the Titanic and the band was playing in the lounge. My aunt was cold so she went inside to listen to the band.

⑦

(8) The passengers and crew were waiting for the captain to give orders. There were so many people, and it was very confusing.

(10) No one wanted to go. I saw a lady in a green coat. She was crying and holding her baby tightly. Her husband kissed them both and said goodbye. Then, she got in the lifeboat and sat down, and they rowed away.

12 *Then, it was our turn. We were waiting in line when a man pushed in front of us. He was very frightened and was shouting. But an officer pulled him away.*

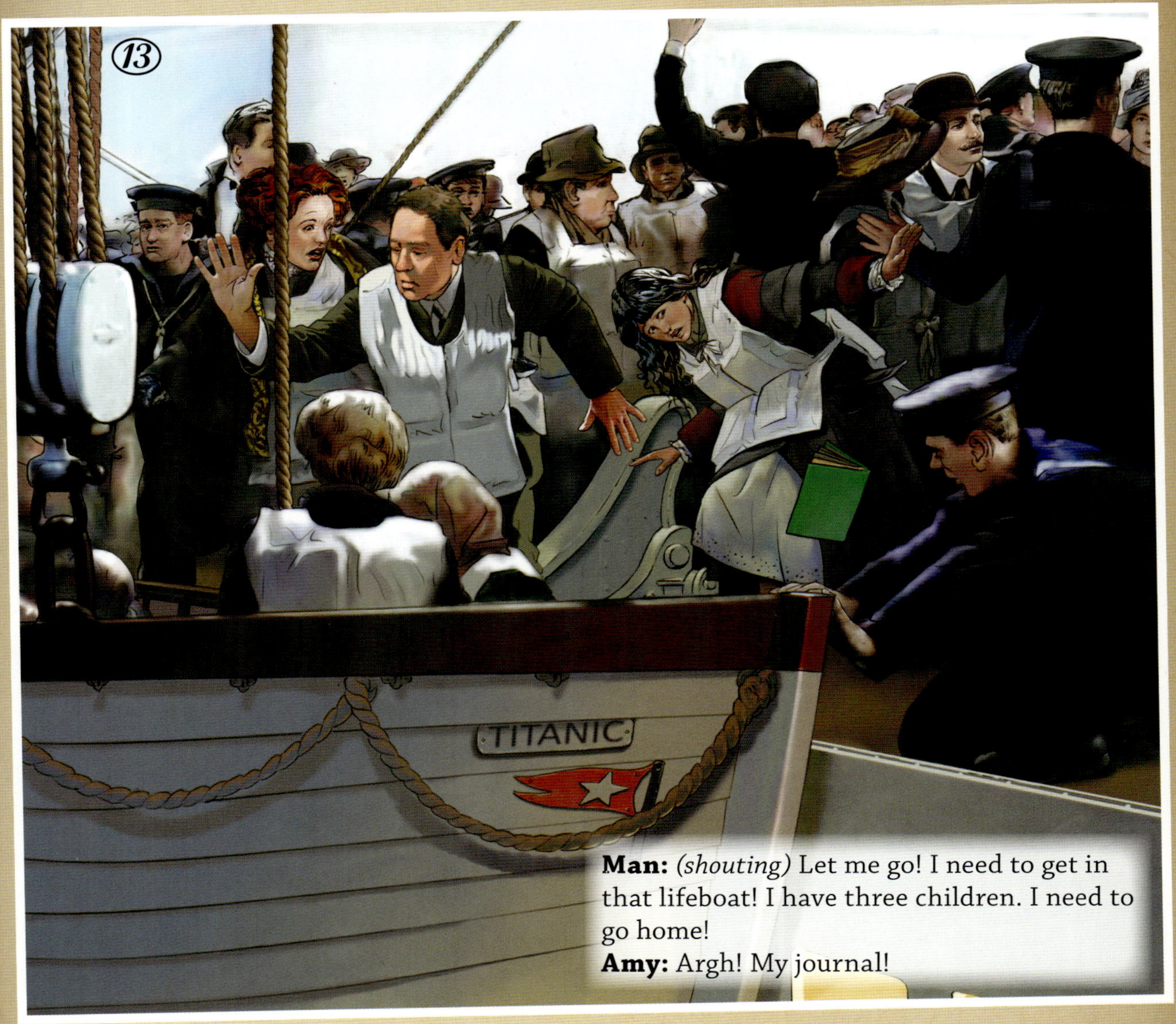

14 *My heart was thumping and my hands were shaking as I climbed into the lifeboat. I looked for Aunt Edith. I didn't want to lose her. A man was helping her down to the boat.*

16

As we sailed away, we watched the ship. The Titanic was sinking into the ocean. The band was still playing. It was dark. The sky was full of stars. Then, everything was silent.

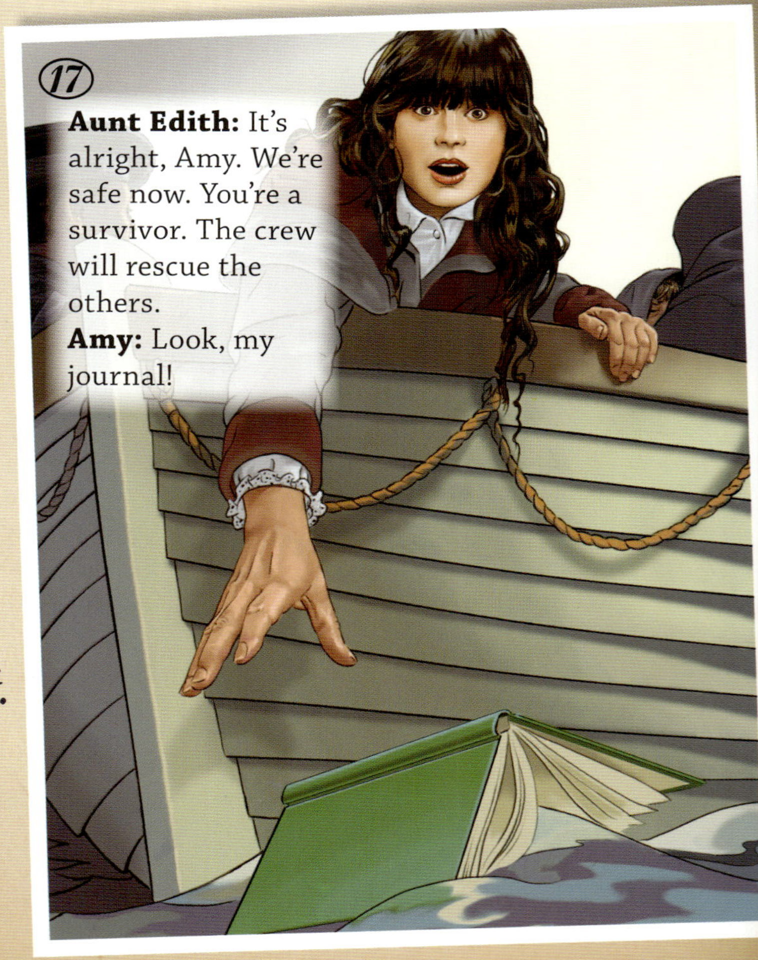

Chapter 7 The Best Food in the World

1

"Rashmi, come quickly! Your brothers are coming home today. Clean the house."

2

Mrs. Kapoor is in the village talking to her neighbor. "My older son, Kuntal, is a chef in the best restaurant in New York. He cooks so well! *And* Shabar makes beautiful cakes for the best bakery in Paris. So smart!
We haven't seen them since Rashmi was little. And, they're cooking for us tonight. Can you imagine it? Two famous chefs in *my* kitchen!"

3

Rashmi is cleaning.

Her mother sits by the door patiently. "They're here!" she shouts suddenly.

Rashmi looks up and sees two men, dressed well.

"Maa!" shout the men, dropping their luggage and greeting their mother.

"Rashmi, you've grown!" says Kuntal.

4

5 Later...

"Don't get in the way, Rashmi," says Kuntal.

"Sorry, I'm just making ..."

"*We're* cooking dinner!" says Shabar.

6

"Look, Shabar! I use the best ingredients. This is the most expensive fish in the world."

"What are you making?" asks Shabar.

"It's a delicious curry for Maa," answers Kuntal.

"Anyone can make curry! It's easy!" laughs Shabar.

"This is a special recipe," Kuntal says. "I chop some onions. Then, I slice the fish thinly. I then fry them quickly in some oil. I mix pepper and spices with coconut milk and cook it very slowly. Finally, I carefully add some fish eggs ... and a piece of real gold. Maa is going to love it."

7

"Well, I'm making a beautiful dessert for Maa," says Shabar.

"It's a tiny bird made from a delicious cookie, on a sugar nest. I boil some water and sugar in a pan. Then, I pour the mixture very carefully to make the nest. I have to do this quickly before the sugar cools. And look! I cut a tiny piece of mango to look like a fish in the bird's beak!"

"Fantastic!" says Kuntal.

"Dinner!" shouts Kuntal.

8

First, Kuntal proudly puts his food on the table. It doesn't look like the curry Maa makes.
"It has *gold* on it!" says Rashmi excitedly.
"It smells good. What is it?" asks Maa.
"It's curry, Maa. You like curry."
She smiles and eats her food. "It needs more pepper."

9

Then, Shabar brings in his dessert.
"I can't eat it," says Maa. "It's too beautiful!"
They eat their meal silently.
Then, Rashmi says, "Maa, I'm still hungry."
"Me, too," says Shabar.
"Let's have the rice pudding that you made, Rashmi," says Maa.
Rashmi brings in a big bowl of hot rice pudding.

10

"Delicious!" says Shabar. "It's so sweet."
"I can smell the saffron," says Kuntal. "It makes me think of home."
"It's wonderful!" says Maa. "It makes me think of my family."
"But," says Kuntal, ... "it just needs a little piece of gold on top!"

11

Chapter 8

GULLIVER IN LILLIPUT

1 My name is Lemuel Gulliver.

I used to be a doctor on a ship, but one day there was a terrible storm. Our ship hit some rocks and sank. The crew drowned. I was alone. So I swam. I swam until I reached an island, where I crawled onto the beach and fell asleep.

2 When I woke up, I heard noises. But I couldn't move. My arms and legs were tied to the ground with ropes. Then something climbed up my leg – a tiny man! Suddenly, forty more men appeared on my chest. I shouted loudly and pulled one hand free, but someone shouted "Tolgo phonac!" I didn't know what it meant, but hundreds of tiny arrows flew at me. So I decided to lie still.

3 Later, while I was sleeping, they moved me to a temple and chained me to the wall. The emperor came to see me, but I couldn't understand him. I pointed to my mouth. He understood and asked his men to bring food.

4 I stayed in Lilliput for nine months. Six hundred people took care of me. They made me clothes, shared their food, and taught me their language. At first they were afraid of me, but when I could speak well, they asked where I came from. I answered that I was from England, but they only knew Lilliput and Blefuscu, a nearby island. They joked that they thought I fell from the stars. I laughed!

5 I asked the emperor to set me free. He told me to be patient. Then he asked me to agree to some rules. I respected him so I agreed, and he told his men to release me.

6 He explained that Lilliput was at war with Blefuscu. Lilliputians argued that eggs should be broken at the small end, but Blefuscudians disagreed. They broke theirs at the big end. They just couldn't agree. He wanted me to capture the Blefuscudian ships. I did this and pulled them back to Lilliput. It wasn't easy; I was attacked with arrows along the way.

7 Then the emperor wanted to capture the Blefuscudian people. I couldn't agree with this and didn't offer to help. He became angry. I knew I was in danger and needed to escape, so I swam to Blefuscu where I found an old boat. Thousands of Blefuscudians helped me drag it onto the beach and repair it. Finally, the boat was ready. They gave me animals for food, and I sailed away.

8

After two days, I saw your ship. You asked where I came from. I told you my story, but you didn't believe me. Here are some tiny animals from Blefuscu. Now do you believe me?

I am Lemuel Gulliver, and this is the truth.

Chapter 9

The Memory Bank

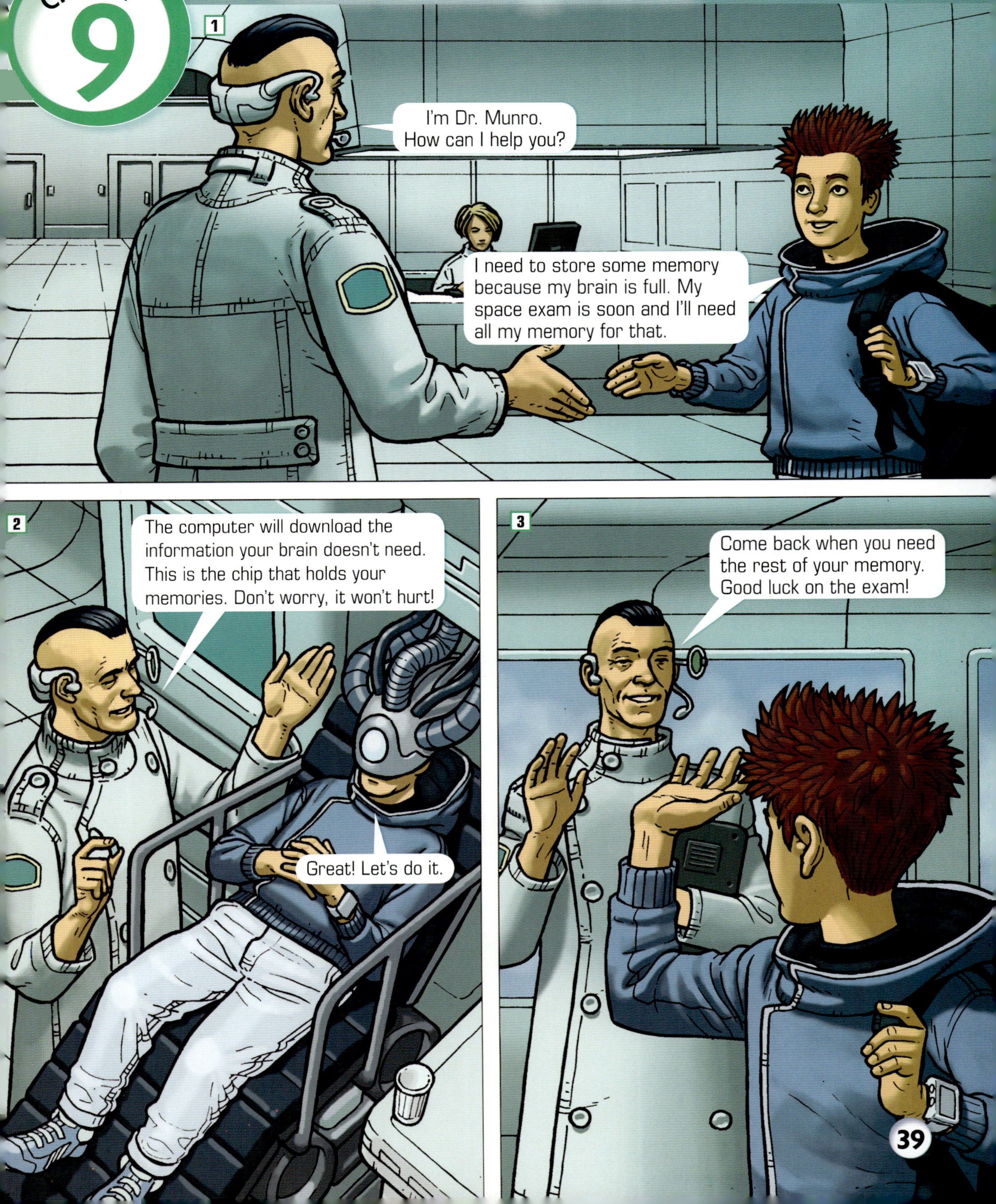

4
This is no good. I can't remember where I live!
5
HOME
OK
6
Hi, Dax, what's the matter?
Where do we live?
Take the K2 – that's the sky tram that goes to Kepler Village. We live in Building 17, downtown.

7
Later...
But Dax, you love pancakes, remember?
No, I don't remember. I know how long it takes to travel to different solar systems, though!
8
That Thursday...
Mom, I'm on the bike path. Where am I taking the exam?
The building is called the Meteor Space Academy. Good luck! You won't need it! You're a great student, remember?
Um ...
9
A few weeks later...
An A+!
Aaargh!

10
Mia, are you OK?
I'm so sorry.
My head.
I think you're OK, but you need to rest at home.
She's taking her exam next week. She'll fail, and it's all my fault.
11
I'd like my old memories back now. You can download some of my exam information to the chip. I don't need it ... but can I share that information with a friend?
12
The next day...
Come with me to see Dr. Munro.
Who's he?
He's the doctor who works at the memory bank.

13
Will I get an A+, too?
You'll have all the information, but
you might remember it differently.

14
But that's cheating!
I feel bad.
Don't worry.
Let's get a drink.

15
THE SHAKE SHACK
SHAKE SHACK
Seaweed shake, please.
That's my favorite, too!

16
I like to sit here. There's no pollution here so there's a lot of wildlife.
So do I. Cool! We like the same things.

17
When I was young, I used to walk my dog, Apollo, here because there was no traffic. What a great dog!

18
Oh, no, Apollo was *my* dog! I think we should go see Dr. Munro.

19
Um, it's bad news. There was a problem with the computer. Some of your old memories were saved on the chip we gave Mia. Dax, your memory is growing on her brain! We need to erase it completely or she will lose all of her own memory, forever.
20
It's OK. I'll just learn everything again and take the exam next year.
21
Will she remember me, Doctor?
I don't know. She might forget *everything*.

22
How are you feeling?
I'm OK, Dax.
You remember me!
Of course. You're the boy who knocked me over! Come on! Let's get a seaweed shake.
23
We won't use this again.

Macmillan Education
4 Crinan Street
London N1 9XW
A division of Macmillan Publishers Limited

Companies and representatives throughout the world

ISBN 978-0-230-45239-8
Pack ISBN 978-0-230-45233-6

Written by Viv Lambert ELT Limited and Mo Choy Design Ltd

First published 2015

Page design and art editing by Wild Apple Design Ltd
Storyboard layouts by Carrie Webb (Red Phoenix Design)
A Boy Named Edward illustrated by Mike Love (Bright Agency); Andy and Grant illustrated by Sanjay Charlton (Beehive Illustration); Down the Rabbit Hole illustrated by Alberto Arzeni (Advocate Art); The Great Balloon Adventure illustrated by Dante Ginerva (Advocate Art); This Strange Land illustrated by Pedro Bascon (Advocate Art); The Journal illustrated by Roy Knipe (Good Illustration); The Best Food in the World illustrated by Victor Tavares (Beehive Illustration); Gulliver in Lilliput illustrated by Fabio Leone (Bright Agency); The Memory Bank illustrated by Paul McCaffery (Sylvie Poggio Artist Agency).
Cover design by Wild Apple Design Ltd
Cover artwork: front cover, Pedro Bascon (Advocate Art), Dante Ginerva (Advocate Art), and Paul McCaffery (Sylvie Poggio Artist Agency); back cover, Sanjay Charlton (Beehive Illustration) and Roy Knipe (Good Illustration).

Authors' acknowledgements
Thank you to everyone at Macmillan for their support and for allowing us to work in 'our way'. For patience and tolerance of late-night working, thank you to our families.

Printed and bound in Thailand

2019 2018 2017 2016
10 9 8 7 6 5 4

Story Central

Student Book 5

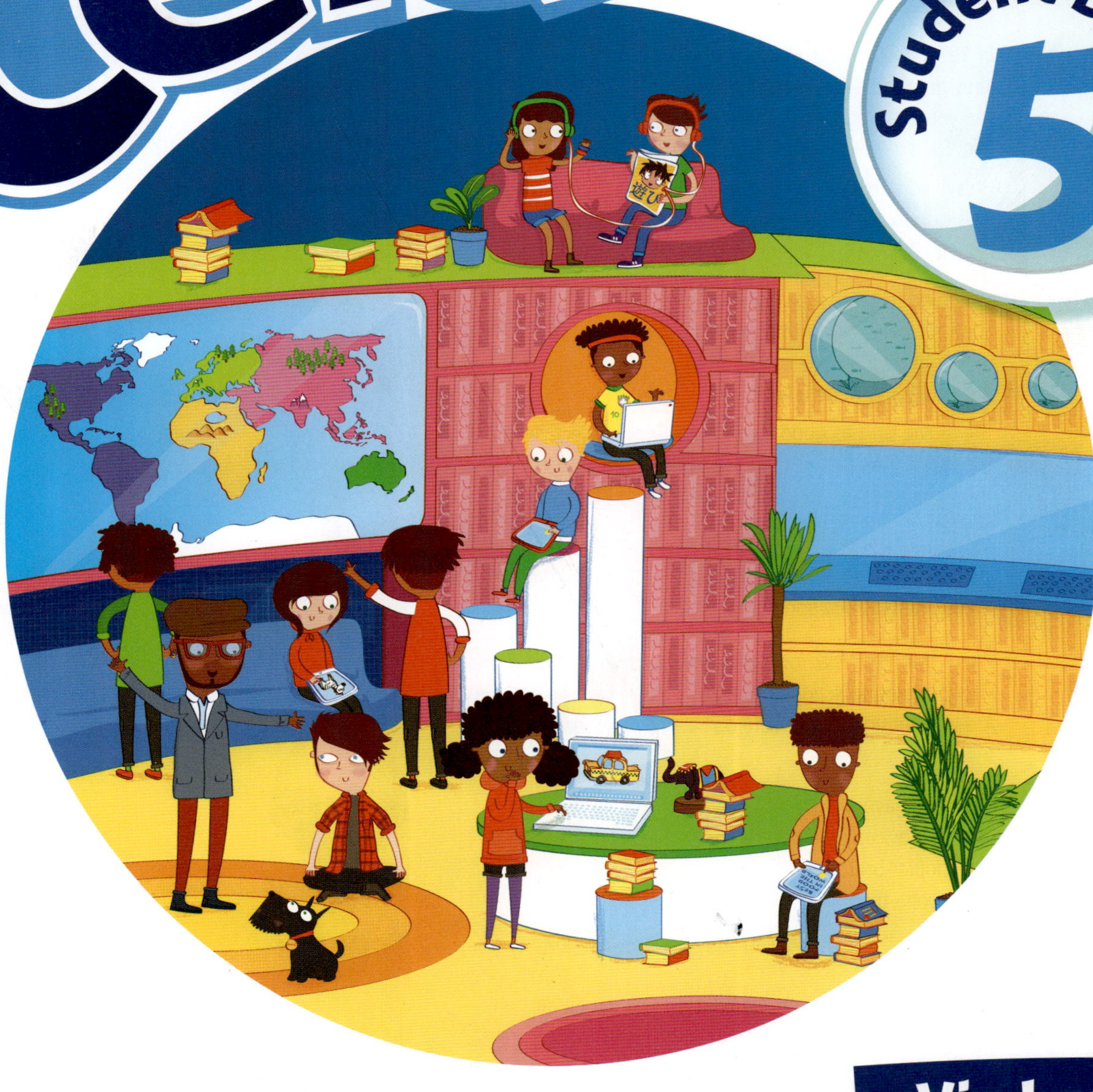

Viv Lambert
Mo Choy

macmillan education

Contents

Competencies

me	act	think	learn	communicate
Activities that encourage children to accept responsibility and reflect on the consequences of lifestyle choices.	Activities that develop societal understanding and identification of children's own circumstances in a wider context.	Activities that develop critical thinking skills to reflect upon, manipulate, process, and interpret information.	Activities that foster learner autonomy, and allow children to demonstrate and put into practice learning strategies.	Activities that promote interpersonal and collaborative skills, develop teamwork, and allow children to express opinions and ideas.

Story Central

1 Listen and read.

The Place to Be!

Story Central is the place to be!
With books to read and friends to see.

When you open a book, you open a door,
To a place you've never been before.

Stories of travel, stories of love.
Stories about the planets above.

Scary stories, stories that are true.
Funny stories, poems, too!

Stories that are new, stories that are old.
Stories that your grandma told.

Stories you remember for the rest of your life.
Stories that paint pictures in your mind.

A book is a journey to another world.
A journey through pages, pictures, and words.

Read it, share it, keep it to yourself.
There are so many stories on the book shelf!

Where Have You Been?

1 **Listen. What did Angelo, Rufus, and Yasmin do for vacation? Write T (true) or F (false).**

1 Angelo visited his grandma. ☐

2 Angelo has been to Italy before. ☐

3 Rufus went to Canada. ☐

4 Rufus saw whales. ☐

5 Yasmin stayed home all vacation. ☐

6 Yasmin visited China. ☐

2 **Where have you been? Where do you want to go? Fill in the form.**

My name's ....

I live in ....

I've been to ....

For vacation, I went to ....

My favorite place is ....

I like traveling by ....

I would like to go to ....

because I like ....

3 **Now listen and match.**

Chapter 1 Then and Now

Lesson 1

1 Listen and check (✔) the things Grandma had.

hula-hoops ☐ dictionaries ☐ computers ☐ an ink pen ☐ a car ☐ desks ☐

2 Listen again and write the words next to the clues.

laptop	~~chalk~~	encyclopedia
interactive whiteboard	ink pen	
chalkboard	hula-hoops	
bell	dictionary	

1 She wrote with ....chalk.... on a ....
2 She brings her computer. It's a ....
3 We look at the .... on the wall.
4 We wrote in our notebooks with an ....
5 We use a .... to check spelling.
6 We use an .... to check facts.
7 She rang a big loud .... for recess.
8 The girls played with ....

1 Read. How was school different in the past?

Did you know …?

There were only two classrooms.
There was a chalkboard and chalk in each classroom.
Children of all ages were in the same class.
The girls and boys had to sit separately.
The girls wore dresses and the boys wore shorts.
Children who misbehaved had to stand in the corner.
They studied reading, writing, and math.
They used dictionaries and encyclopedias.
They wrote with ink pens.
Some children didn't go to school. They worked on farms or in factories.

2 Write the verbs in the past tense in two columns in your notebook.

regular	irregular
studied	was/were

be ~~study~~ write use
work wear have to

3 Imagine a dialogue with Molly. Ask and answer. Use the verbs in Activity 2.

"Did they …? Were there …?
Where did …? What did …?"

A: *Did they wear uniforms?*

B: *No, they didn't. The boys wore shorts and the girls wore dresses.*

Grammar Central

Simple past

They ...studied... reading, writing, and math.
The boys and girls .... sit separately.
.... the girls .... dresses?
Yes, they ....
What .... they .... with?
They .... with ink pens.

Lesson 3

Telling Stories

1 **Listen and read.**

2 **Talk to a friend about first grade.**

"my teacher
my classroom
my best friend
my first day"

A: *Do you remember first grade?*

B: *Yes, I do. I remember my teacher. Her name was Miss Gray.*

A BOY NAMED EDWARD

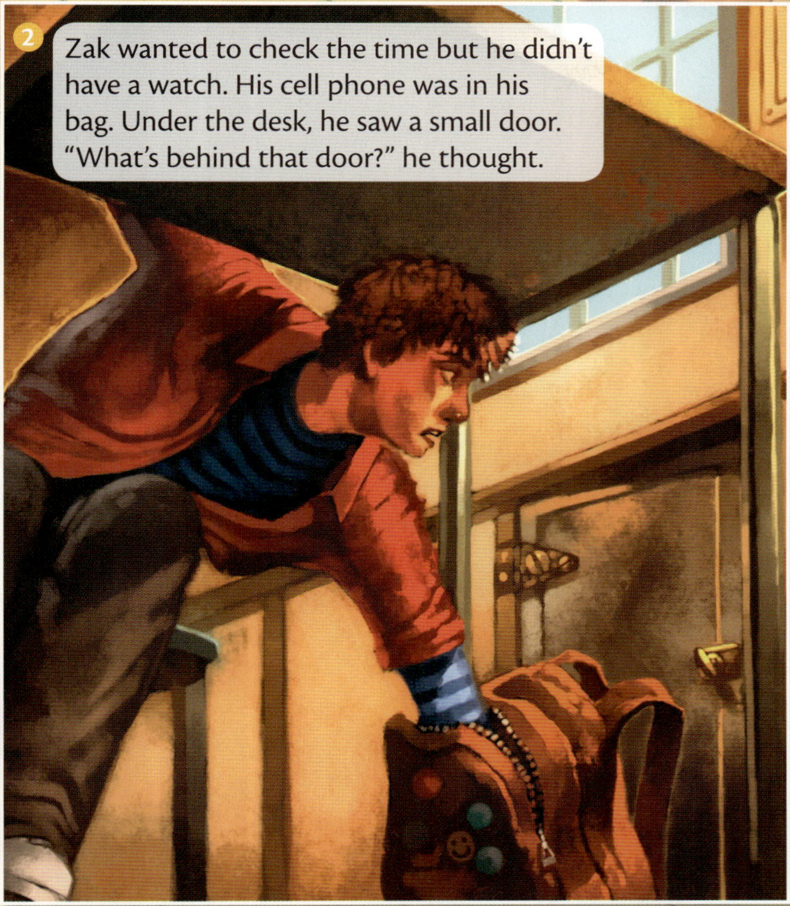

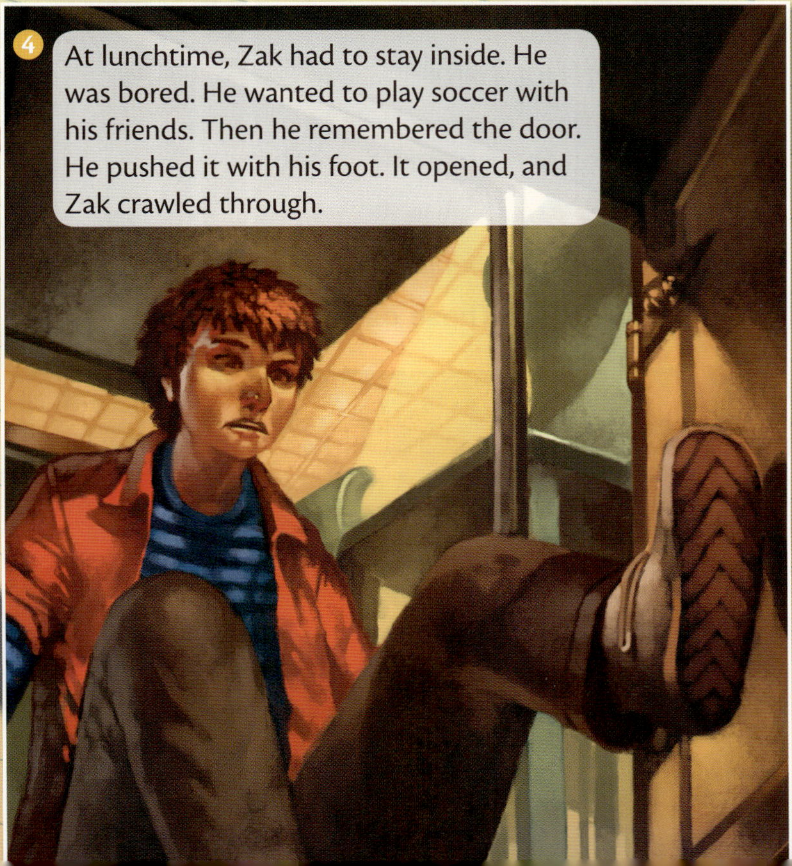

STORY

3 Look at the story. Who do you think is the boy named Edward?

4 Read the story extract and answer.

1 Why did Zak have to stay inside at lunchtime?

---

2 How do you think Zak feels about Mr. Cunningham?

---

3 What type of story is this? Why do you think this?

Lesson 4

Time to Think

1 **Read the story in your Reader.**

Did you guess who Edward was? What were the clues?

2 **Comprehension**

1 What time was lunch at Edward's school?

---

2 Why did the boys laugh at Edward?

---

3 How did Mr. Cunningham know it was his cap?

---

4 Why are some of the pictures in this story in color and others in black and white?

---

3 **Critical Literacy**

1 Would you like to go to school now or in the past?
2 How do you think Zak felt about the school he visited in the past?

Writing Workshop Comparing the past and present.

4 **Imagine your classroom 60 years ago. Write about the difference between then and now. Give your opinions.**

In the old days, students had to sit separately. Today, we can sit together. I think that's good because I like working with other people ...

Writing Tools

Use time expressions to write about the past and present:

In the past, ... **In 19 ______, ...**

Before, ... *In the old days, ...*

Today, ... These days, ... Now, ...

5 **Text Connections**

Do you know any other stories about time travel from books or movies?

Lesson 5

1 **Listen and read. Was Scarlett's school like Edward's school in the past?**

Scarlett: Did you like that story?

Yasmin: Yes, I did. I'd love to travel back in time.

Scarlett: Me, too.

Angelo: I used to have an imaginary friend, just like Edward. I used to talk to him in my room.

Yasmin: Ha, ha! That's funny!

Scarlett: You know, our school used to be like Edward's many years ago. My mom told me. There were chalkboards and chalk. The boys used to wear shorts. There weren't any computers.

Angelo: Did the children use to have lunch at school?

Scarlett: No, they used to go home for lunch. And they didn't use to have pizza and fries!

Yasmin: Did you ever have to stay in at lunchtime, Rufus?

Rufus: No way! I was a good student.

2 **Circle *used to* or *didn't use to*.**

1 Angelo *used to* / *didn't use to* have an imaginary friend.
2 The boys *used to* / *didn't use to* wear shorts.
3 They *used to* / *didn't use to* have computers.
4 The children *used to* / *didn't use to* have lunch at home.
5 Rufus *used to* / *didn't use to* be a good student.

3 **Talk to a friend about what you used to do.**

play with   like   have   do   talk to   be

A: *I used to play with dolls. Did you use to have an imaginary friend?*

B: *No, I didn't, but I used to talk to my teddy bear.*

Grammar Central

***used to* + verb**

In 1950, the boys used to wear shorts.
They ______ have computers.
Did you ______ have lunch at school when you were young?
Yes, we ______. / No, we ______.

Lesson 6

SONG

1 **Listen and sing. How is Grandpa speaking to his grandson?**

That's How We Talk!

When I was young, my friends and I met.
*Now we have cell phones and we **text**.*
We used to talk and go for a walk.
*We **chat online**. That's how we talk!*

We used to play soccer in the park.
I play games online with my friend Mark.
*We listened to **records** by the Rolling Stones.*
*Now people **download** music and use **earphones**.*

I had an encyclopedia of facts.
The Internet's much better than that!
I wrote letters with my favorite ink pen.
*I **type emails**. Then I press "send."*

I can see and talk to you, but you're miles away.
I know, it's so cool, I have so much to say.
*Let's have another **video call** soon.*
OK, Grandpa, I miss you, too.

2 **Talk to a friend about then and now. Use the words from the song.**

A: *In the past, they used to listen to records.*
B: *Now, we download music.*

Spelling Central

Circle the letter in each word that you can't hear.

fr(i)ends when talk walk

Write the words and their silent letters in the chart. Can you add more silent letter words?

word	silent letter
friends	i

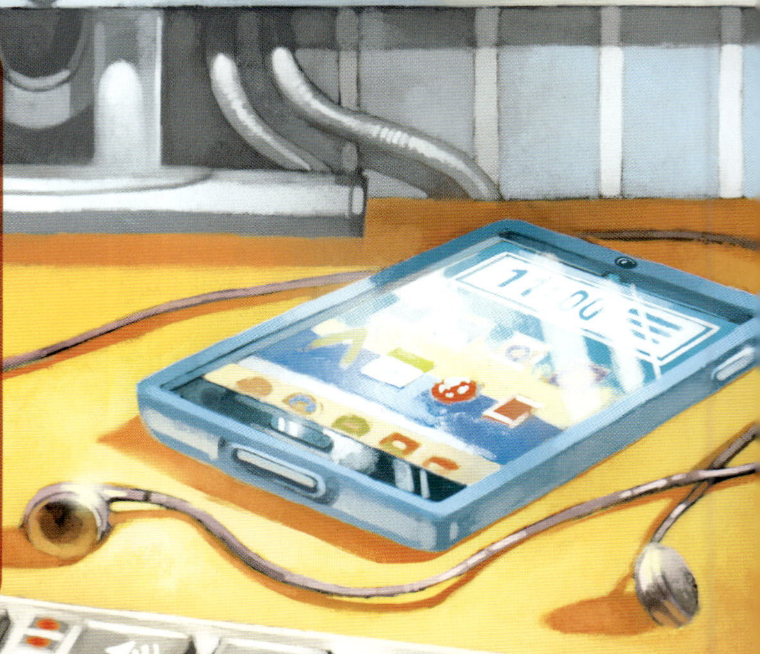

1 Read. What is a time capsule?

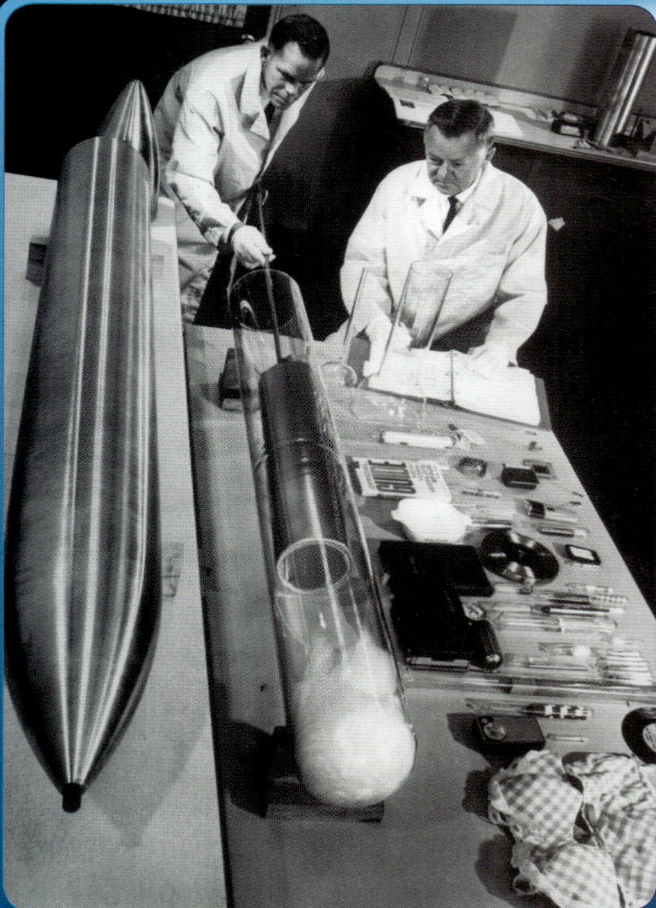

Time Capsules

A time capsule has different things in it to show how people used to live in the past. It's like a little museum in a box! People usually bury time capsules in the ground, but there are also some time capsules in space.

In 1939, the Westinghouse Time Capsule was created as a message to the future. It was shown at the New York World's Fair before being buried. It still lies under the ground. It contains many things, including a telephone, a camera, money, plant seeds, a dictionary, and also photographs, movies, records, and magazines. There's even a letter from the famous scientist Albert Einstein, written in his ink pen.

This time capsule is buried in a secret place. In many libraries around the world, there is a book with a map of where to find the time capsule and instructions on how to open it in 5,000 years.

2 Write T (true) or F (false).

1 Time capsules are sometimes sent into space. T
2 There's a cell phone in the Westinghouse Time Capsule. ☐
3 Albert Einstein typed a letter which is in the time capsule. ☐
4 Nobody knows where the Westinghouse Time Capsule is buried. ☐
5 The Westinghouse Time Capsule should be opened in 6939. ☐

3 Discuss.

Is it important to remember the past? Why? / Why not?

4 Find Out More!

What are the most interesting and useful things that have been put in a time capsule? What shouldn't you put in?

Search Engine

When you're searching for advice it's good to compare ideas. Find out what different people put in their time capsules.

PROJECT

Lesson 8

Prepare

1 In groups, talk about a time and place in the past.

In 19...... , they didn't …
In the old days, people …
When my mom was young, she …
My grandpa used to …

Write

2 Write a Time Travel story.

- Choose a time and place.
- Draw a picture.
- Write a paragraph describing what and who you saw.

Writing Tools

When you describe the setting for a time travel story:

Use the simple past and the past progressive tenses.

Story Central Level 5 Chapter 1 Lesson 8

Time Travel Story

Time: 1975
Place: Old house
What did you see? clock, TV, radio
Who did you meet? a woman.
What were they wearing? an orange dress
What did they say? "This is my daughter"
How did you feel? excited, happy

I opened the door. It was 1975. I saw a clock on the wall. It was my grandma's house. There was a big black and white TV but there wasn't a computer. I met a woman who was wearing an orange dress. She had a baby girl. The woman said, "This is my daughter Susan." I was excited. Susan is my mom's name.

Showcase

3 Present your Time Travel story setting to the class.

Reflect

4 Vote for the best Time Travel story and talk to the class.

I liked it because it was exciting.

I liked it when he opened the door and saw his old bedroom.

1 Listen and write the missing words.

1 Zak ......wore...... long pants and he had ....very different.... hair.
2 That day, they .... find out about ancient temples.
3 Edward had a big .... on his desk.
4 Edward didn't have a .... in those days.
5 Those boys .... chase Edward every day.
6 He lost his .... and never found it.

2 Write sentences in your notebook about the picture. Use *used to* or *didn't use to* with these verbs.

listen to   have   play   read
chat online   download   wear

In the past, they ...
In the 1950s, children ...

3 Think about Chapter 1. Color the bone.

Which activity was easy? ....

Which activity was difficult? ....

Figure it out with a friend.

Write a tip to help you remember.
....
....

Treasure Hunt!

Look back at pages 4 and 5.

Where was the Westinghouse Time Capsule shown? Find the city on the map.

Find something from that city. What is it?

Chapter 2 Work Hard, Play Hard!

Lesson 1

1 Listen and write the day and the time.

School clubs

Karate lessons
Take karate lessons with Sensei Sam. Wear comfortable clothes and bring a bottle of water.
Saturday morning in the gym.

Chess club
Come and play chess. Small, friendly chess club. All ages welcome. It's the game to exercise your brain!
________ in Room 6.

Photography club
Digital photography class. Learn to take great pictures. Beginners welcome.
____
Meet in the cafeteria.

Writing workshop
Write stories and poetry with help from a published author!
____
Room 11.

Cooking club
Learn to bake cakes. Ask Mrs. Matthews for this week's recipe. Week 1: chocolate cake. We love baking! ________ in the kitchen.

Japanese club
Learning Japanese with Akio is easy and fun. ________
Mr. Brown's classroom.

2 Listen again and write the words next to the clues.

~~baking~~ Japanese photography poetry karate chess

1 You use your hands and feet a lot. ________

2 You have to think carefully. ________

3 You don't need a camera. ________

4 You just follow a recipe. baking

5 You have to have a good imagination. ________

6 You have to learn a new alphabet. ________

1 Read. What are Peter's hobbies?

KARATE KID

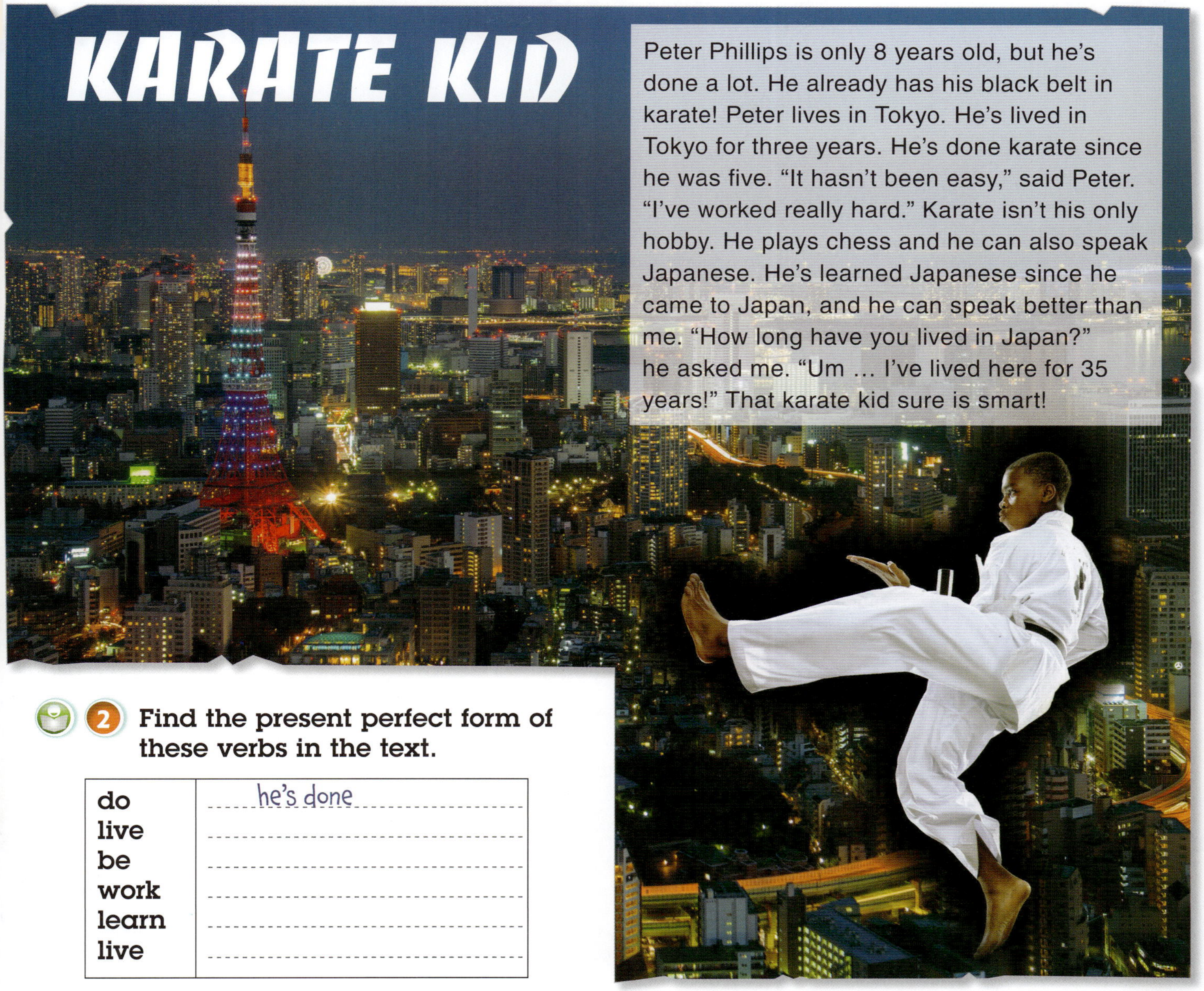

Peter Phillips is only 8 years old, but he's done a lot. He already has his black belt in karate! Peter lives in Tokyo. He's lived in Tokyo for three years. He's done karate since he was five. "It hasn't been easy," said Peter. "I've worked really hard." Karate isn't his only hobby. He plays chess and he can also speak Japanese. He's learned Japanese since he came to Japan, and he can speak better than me. "How long have you lived in Japan?" he asked me. "Um … I've lived here for 35 years!" That karate kid sure is smart!

2 Find the present perfect form of these verbs in the text.

do	he's done
live	
be	
work	
learn	
live	

3 Imagine a dialogue with Peter. Ask and answer. Use the verbs in Activity 2.

"How old …? How long …?
Can you …? What …?"

A: *How long have you lived in Tokyo?*

B: *I've lived here for three years / since I was five.*

Grammar Central

Present perfect: *for* and *since*

I 've lived here for 35 years.

He's lived here ______ three years.

How long ______ you ______ in Japan?

I've lived here ______ I was five.

Lesson 3

Telling Stories

1 Listen and read.

2 **Tell a friend why you haven't seen them in a long time.**

"I've been away.
I've been sick.
I've been at …
I've been busy."

A: *Hey, Mandy. I haven't seen you for ages!*

B: *I know. I've been away on vacation.*

Andy and Grant

1

"I've been here for months," said Grant. "I've slept a lot and enjoyed the sun. I wanted to learn how to play chess, but the ants don't want to play with me. So, I've read some poetry, in Japanese! I've done some photography and … hey! I've written a song. Listen. I might learn some karate next!"

3

"Ants are so stupid," Grant thought. "I've relaxed in the sun every day since the spring. I've never wasted time working in the summer."

"When are you going to stop?" asked Grant.

"We're going to stop in the fall when we've collected all the corn. Ants have lived in this field for many years. We've collected corn all summer, every summer, for hundreds of years. It's what ants do!"

"Yes, yes, you're very smart," said Andy. "And I'm very busy." He picked up the corn and carried it to a hole in the ground.

"You should relax more," said Grant. "There's plenty of food right now." Grant pulled a leaf from a plant and ate it.

STORY

3 Look at the story. What season do you think it is?

4 Read the story extract and answer.

1 What are Grant's hobbies?

---

2 What do you think is going to happen in the winter?

---

3 What are the insects in the story similar to?

Lesson 4

Time to Think

1 **Read the story in your Reader.**

Which insect is smarter?

2 **Comprehension**

1 Why has Andy worked all summer?

---

2 What's Grant done all summer?

---

3 How long have ants worked in the field?

---

4 Does Andy help Grant at the end?

---

3 **Critical Literacy**

1 Do you think Andy was right not to help Grant?
2 Are you an ant or a grasshopper? Why?

Writing Workshop Writing about what you've done.

4 **Think about what your hobbies are, and how long you've done them. Write about your hobbies.**

I've played ...	I've learned ...
I've done ...	I've practiced ...

I've played soccer for four years.

Writing Tools

Use these time expressions with *since*:

2010 last summer
last month I was five

Use these time expressions with *for*:

three years six weeks
two months a long time

5 **Text Connections**

What do you learn from this story?

Lesson 5

BOOK CLUB

1 Listen and read. What jobs are Angelo and Yasmin going to do?

Angelo: I loved Grant's music. I'm going to go to music school.

Yasmin: You might not get into music school.

Angelo: I'm going to work really hard. Who knows? I might be a famous pop star one day!

Yasmin: Ha, ha! Oh, yeah? You aren't going to be famous!

Angelo: Don't laugh. It might take a long time, but you might see me on TV.

Scarlett: What are you going to do, Yasmin? Are you going to be a doctor?

Yasmin: Hm, I don't know. I'm not going to go to college right after school. I might travel for a year first. Then I might study to be a vet. Or I might be a singer and join your band, Angelo.

Angelo: Oh, no!

2 Write about the characters' future plans.

Definite plans	Possible actions
Angelo is going to go to music school. *He's going to work really hard.*	*He might be famous.*

3 Talk to a friend about your weekend plans.

"*I'm going to … I'm not going to … I might … I might not …*"

A: *What are you going to do this weekend?*

B: *I'm going to play soccer on Saturday. What about you?*

A: *Oh! I don't know, I might come and watch.*

Grammar Central

going to* and *might

I'm *going to* go to music school.
She isn't .... go to college.
He .... be a singer.
Are you .... be a vet?

Lesson 6

SONG

1 **Listen and sing. What is the most important thing?**

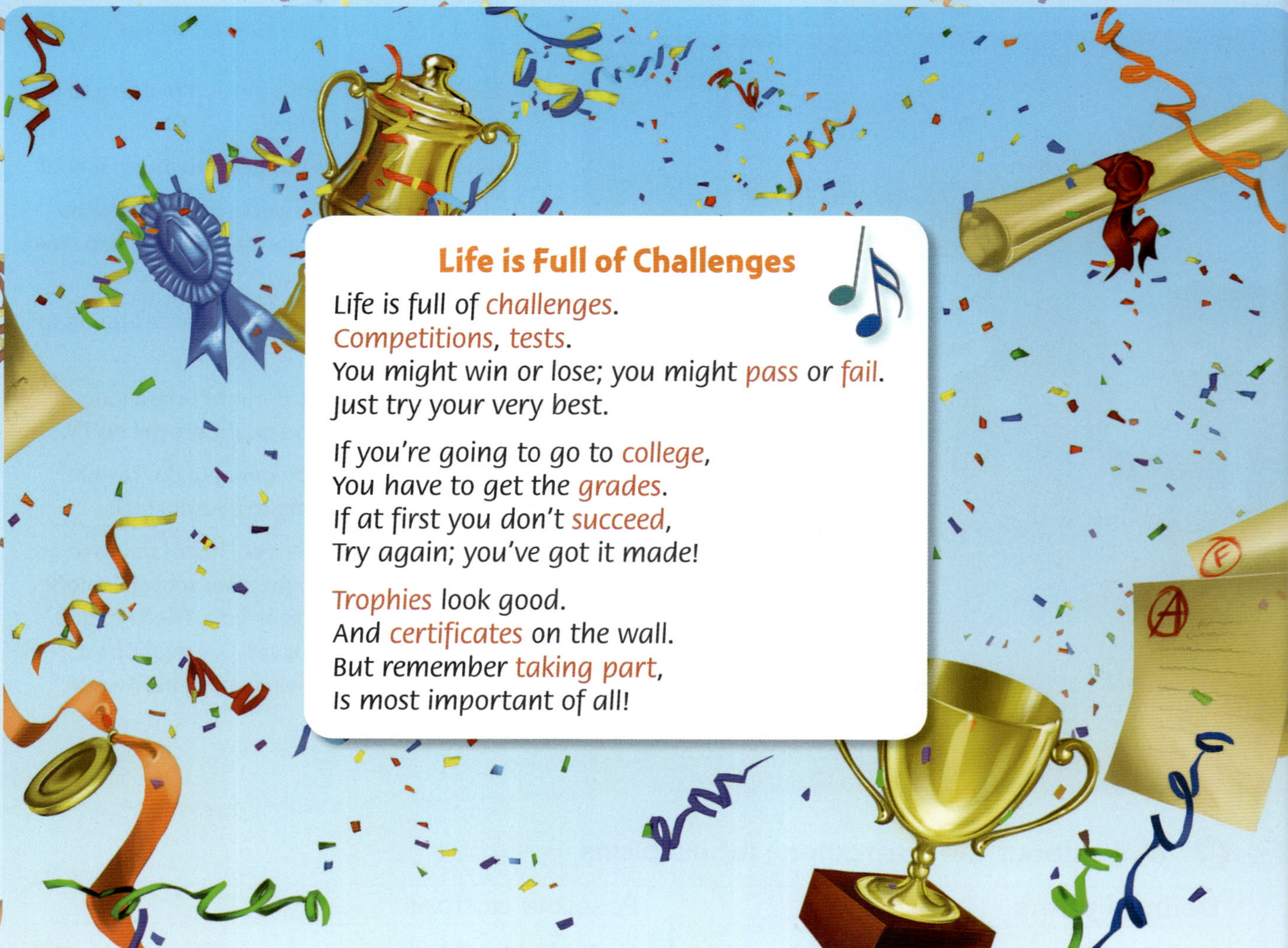

Life is Full of Challenges

Life is full of challenges.
Competitions, tests.
You might win or lose; you might pass or fail.
Just try your very best.

If you're going to go to college,
You have to get the grades.
If at first you don't succeed,
Try again; you've got it made!

Trophies look good.
And certificates on the wall.
But remember taking part,
Is most important of all!

2 **Talk to a friend about your past and future. Use the words from the song.**

Have you ever ...? *I've ... I haven't ...*
I might ... *I want to ...*
Are you going to ...?

A: *Have you ever won a competition?*

B: *No, I haven't. I'm going to take part in a dance competition. I might win!*

Spelling Central

Circle the words with double consonants *ll*.

Write the words in the chart. Can you add more *ll* words?

***ll* at the end**	***ll* in the middle**
full	

1 Read. What activities might you do on an expedition?

Taking On a Challenge

It's tough deciding what to do after school. Maybe you failed your exams or you just want to take a break. Here are some ideas for new challenges you can do before you go to college or start looking for a job.

If you like traveling, you might like to go on an expedition. For example, you might travel to Borneo, Costa Rica, or Tanzania and stay in small villages with the local people there. It isn't a vacation! You might take part in community projects like helping a village get clean water and electricity. You might help build a school and teach young children to read. You won't be paid money for working. You are a volunteer.

You aren't going to come home with a trophy or a certificate, but you're going to learn a lot about the world, and about yourself. You'll be stronger and have better ideas about what you want to do with your life. You might decide to take more exams and go to college or you might decide you want to travel more and be a volunteer with a charity. Whatever you decide, the experience is going to change your life.

2 Write T (true) or F (false).

1 You don't have to go to college after school. T

2 An expedition is a vacation to another country. ☐

3 You might work in a school. ☐

4 The local people pay you well. ☐

5 You're going to get a certificate after the expedition. ☐

3 Discuss.

Do you want to go on a charity expedition? Why? / Why not?

4 Find Out More!

Find out what your community needs. How can you help?

Search Engine

Search for local charities and community groups. They have a lot of information about what's needed in your community.

Lesson 8

PROJECT

Prepare

1 In groups, talk about your achievements and goals.

"I've … since I was …
I've … for … years / months
I passed / won … in July / 2012
I'm going to …"

Write

2 Make a 'My Life' vision board.

- Collect and draw some pictures. Choose some headings.
- Write sentences about your achievements and goals.

What have you already achieved?
What are you going to do in the future?
What might you do?

Writing Tools

When you write a vision board:

Use *going to* and *might* to talk about your goals.
Use the present perfect and simple past tenses to talk about your achievements.

Showcase

3 Present your vision board to the class.

Reflect

4 Vote for the best vision boards.

I think … is cool because she's going to travel to Australia.

I might be a singer, too!

1 Listen and match. Then write T (true) or F (false).

dad | friend | brother

1 She's baked cakes for eight years. F
2 Her brother has won baking competitions. ___
3 She's learned Japanese. ___
4 Her dad has played chess since he was young. ___
5 Her brother has been at college for two years. ___
6 She's never made a cake for her mom. ___

2 Write sentences in your notebook about your future. Use *going to* / *not going to* or *might* / *might not* with these verbs.

go to college   pass my exams
be a teacher   work   travel

When I'm 18, I'm going to...
After school, I might...

3 Think about Chapter 2. Color the bone.

Which activity was easy? ____________

Which activity was difficult? ____________

Figure it out with a friend.

Write a tip to help you remember.
____
____

Treasure Hunt!

Look back at pages 4 and 5.

Where has Peter lived for three years? Find the city on the map.

Find something from that country. What is it?

Chapter 3 Sleep and Dreams

Lesson 1

1 Listen and number the dreams in the order you hear them.

Six most common dreams

Have you ever had a dream about …

falling? ☐

going out in your pajamas? ☐

flying? ☐

your teeth falling out? ☐

being late for school? ☐

being chased? 1

2 Listen again and write the words next to the clues.

disappointing amazing realistic ~~frightening~~ confusing awful weird embarrassing

1 I was really scared.
frightening

2 My face was red and I wanted to hide.
....

3 I couldn't understand what was happening.
....

4 I had to look in the mirror to see if it was true.
....

5 My dream was awesome!
....

6 I wasn't so happy at the end.
....

7 I felt so bad.
....

8 It was strange.
....

1 Read. What's the name of the author?

Movie Review: Alice in Wonderland

About the Movie

The movie tells a story about a young girl's amazing dream. Alice's dream takes place in an imaginary world called Wonderland. She meets the same weird and wonderful characters that she meets in the book and she has the same awesome adventures. The movie isn't as confusing as the book by Lewis Carroll because the plot is easier to follow.

Send us your comments.

The movie isn't as good as the book. (Jake, 12, USA)

I think the movie is better than the book, but the movie's more frightening. (Eleanor, 10, England)

The dream is more amazing in the movie. (Helena, 11, Spain)

I thought the movie was disappointing. (Tom, 11, France)

I think the movie is just as good as the book. (Izzy, 13, USA)

The plot was awful. The movie wasn't as exciting as the book. (Pablo, 14, Mexico)

The characters in the book aren't as realistic as the characters in the movie. (Sam, 11, Canada)

2 Read again. Find the phrases in the text that mean the same.

1 The book is better than the movie. The movie isn't as good as the book.
2 The book isn't as good as the movie. ________
3 The book isn't as frightening as the movie. ________
4 The book was more exciting than the movie. ________
5 The book is just as good as the movie. ________

3 Talk to a friend. Compare a movie and a book.

"more interesting than / better than / not as exciting as / just as good as"

A: Do you like movies or books?
B: I like books. They're more interesting than movies.
A: I like movies. They aren't as confusing as books.

Grammar Central

than* / (*not*) *as* (adjective) *as* / *just as* (adjective) *as

The movie isn't as good as the book. = The book is ________ than the movie.

The book wasn't as ________ as the movie. = The movie was scarier ________ the book.

Lesson 3

Telling Stories

1 Listen and read.

2 Ask a friend about their dreams.

> flying
> being chased
> spiders
> failing a test

A: Have you ever dreamed about being chased?

B: Yes, I have. I often dream about being chased. Have you ever dreamed about flying?

A: Yes, I have. It's amazing!

STORY

3 **Look at the story. When do you think Alice falls asleep?**

4 **Read the story extract and answer.**

1 What happened after Alice saw the white rabbit?

----

2 Where do you think the rabbit hole takes Alice?

----

3 Where does the story take place? Is it a real place or an imaginary place?

Lesson 4
Time to Think

1 **Read the story in your Reader.**

What happens when Alice drinks from the bottle?

2 **Comprehension**

1 Why couldn't Alice go through the door?

---

2 Do you think Alice cried for a long time?

---

3 Why did the rabbit run away from her?

---

4 Do you think the rabbit was real?

---

3 **Critical Literacy**

1 Do you think Alice liked being in Wonderland?
2 Would you like to go to Wonderland?

Writing Workshop Linking parts of a story.

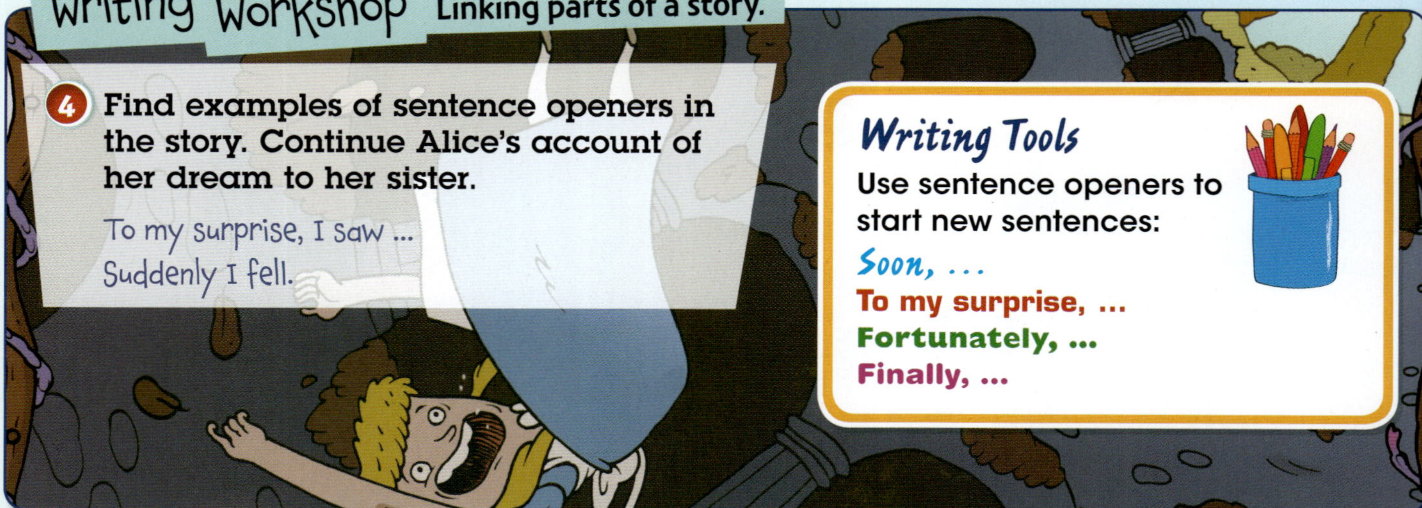

4 **Find examples of sentence openers in the story. Continue Alice's account of her dream to her sister.**

To my surprise, I saw ...
Suddenly I fell.

Writing Tools

Use sentence openers to start new sentences:

Soon, ...
To my surprise, ...
Fortunately, ...
Finally, ...

5 **Text Connections**

Do you know any other stories or movies about people who get bigger or smaller?

Lesson 5

BOOK CLUB

1 Listen and read. What did Angelo dream about?

Yasmin: Last night, I dreamed I could fly. It was an awesome dream. I was so disappointed when I woke up.

Scarlett: Yes, it's disappointing when you wake up from a good dream.

Angelo: I dreamed about a monster.

Yasmin: Oh, this dream is so boring! I've heard it already.

Scarlett: Sh! Yasmin. I'm not bored. I'm interested. Were you frightened, Angelo?

Angelo: Oh, yes! The monster looked really scary – big and ugly. It was frightening.

Scarlett: Well, that's an interesting dream.

Angelo: When I woke up I was shouting, "Mommy, Mommy, help!"

Scarlett: Ha, ha! Did your mom hear you?

Angelo: No, she didn't, but Yasmin heard me. I was so embarrassed!

Scarlett: Yes, that's *really* embarrassing.

2 Circle the correct word.

1 Yasmin was *disappointed* / *disappointing* when she woke up.
2 Yasmin is *bored* / *boring* because she has heard the dream before.
3 The monster in Angelo's dream was *frightened* / *frightening*.
4 Angelo's dream was *interesting* / *interested*.
5 Angelo was *embarrassing* / *embarrassed* because Yasmin heard him.

3 Talk to a friend. Use the adjectives in Activity 2.

A: *I was disappointed when I failed my music exam.*
B: *I was embarrassed when I fell over in P.E.*

Grammar Central

***-ed* / *-ing* adjectives**

The book is boring. I feel ______________.
I'm disappointed. The movie was ______________.

Lesson 6

1 Read. Then listen and match the people to their sleep habits.

When you **lie down** and close your eyes, do you **fall asleep** easily at night? Or do you **stay awake** and think about things? Many people take a teddy bear to bed with them, while others might have a special **pillow**. Do you turn off all the lights or are you frightened of **the dark**? Do you **stay up** late or go to bed early? When you can't sleep, do you count sheep?

Spelling Central

Circle the words that have *-gh* in the text.

Write the words in the chart. Can you add more *-gh* words?

-gh
night

2 **Talk to a friend about your sleep habits. Use the words from the text.**

A: *I lie down and close my eyes. Then I fall asleep.*

B: *I turn off all the lights. I'm not frightened of the dark.*

1 Read. Then complete the quiz. Are you a good sleeper?

Sleep Habits Quiz

The Importance of Sleep

Sleep is very important for your health. We all have a body clock that makes us stay awake in the day and sleep at night. Your body and mind need to turn off at night, and most people need about eight hours of sleep. When you're sick, you need to sleep for longer so that you can get better. Do you have good sleep habits? Take the quiz and find out.

Quiz:

1 Do you go to bed at the same time every day?
a yes **b** no

2 When you can't sleep, do you ...
a get up and read? **b** lie in bed?

3 Do you eat chocolate or drink tea or coffee at night?
a no **b** yes

4 When do you have dinner?
a More than an hour before bed time.
b Less than an hour before bed time.

5 When do you exercise?
a In the day. **b** At night.

6 Do you stay up as late as possible and watch TV or surf the Internet?
a no **b** yes

7 Do you get out of bed when the alarm goes off?
a yes **b** no

8 Are you very tired when you wake up in the morning?
a no **b** yes

9 Do you like a special toy or pillow to help you fall asleep?
a yes **b** no

10 How many hours do you sleep every night?
a More than seven. **b** Less than seven.

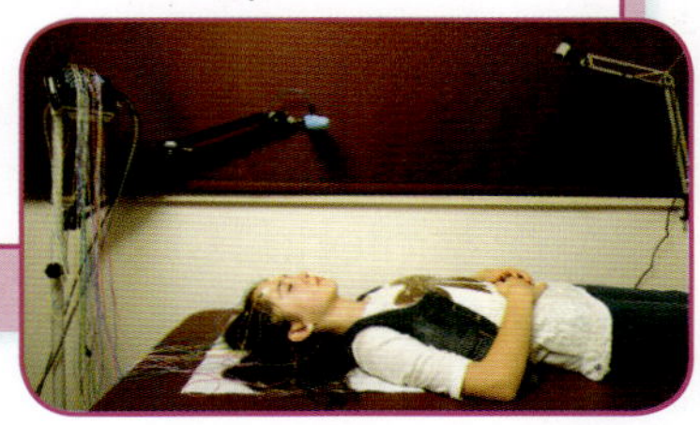

2 Count the *As* and *Bs* then read the results.

Mostly a:
Very good! You have good sleep habits. You're healthy and you get enough sleep.

Mostly b:
You should try to change how you sleep. It's important to have good sleep habits or you might get tired or sick.

3 Discuss.

Should you have a TV or computer in your bedroom? Why? / Why not?

4 Find Out More!

Find out more about body clocks and sleep cycles. What happens to you when you're asleep?

Search Engine

Use keywords together to get better search results, e.g. body clock, sleep cycle.

PROJECT Lesson 8

Prepare

1 In groups, talk about dreams you've had.

> *I once dreamed I was running …*
> *I was frightened.*
> *Have you ever dreamed that …?*
> *It's weird.*
> *My best dream was about …*
> *It was amazing.*

Write

2 **Write an account of a dream.**

- Draw a picture of your dream.
- Write a paragraph about your dream.
  Where were you?
  What was it like?
  What happened?
  How did you feel in the dream and how did you feel when you woke up?

Writing Tools

When you write an account of a dream:
Use the simple past and past progressive tenses.
Use sentence openers to vary the start of sentences.
Use adjectives to describe how you felt.

Showcase

3 **Present your dream account to the class.**

Reflect

4 **Vote for the best account of a dream and talk to the class.**

The best dream was about being late for school.

The dream about falling wasn't as frightening as the one about being chased.

1 Listen and write sentences using *as* … *as* and *more* … *than*.

1 Giant ants / sharks / interesting *Giant ants are more interesting than sharks.*

2 Shark Island / the Angry Ant game / frightening ______________________

3 Angry Ant Adventure / Shark Island / confusing ______________________

4 Sharks / Angry Ants / realistic ______________________

5 Shark Island / Angry Ant Adventure / disappointing ______________________

2 Write sentences in your notebook about a game you've played. Use these words.

confusing / confused   disappointing / disappointed
exciting / excited   boring / bored   interesting / interested

This game is …   I was …   The characters are …

3 Think about Chapter 3. Color the bone.

Which activity was easy? ______

Which activity was difficult? ______

Figure it out with a friend.

Write a tip to help you remember.
____
____

Treasure Hunt!

Look back at pages 4 and 5.

Where is Wonderland? Can you find the place on the map?

Find something from that place. What is it?

Chapter 4 Up and Away!

Lesson 1

1 Listen and label the picture.

~~pilot~~ balloon
hot air basket
ropes

2 Listen again and write the missing words.

passengers land ~~flight~~
safe view takes off

1 Perfect weather for a balloon flight.
2 How many .... do we have today?
3 I undo these long brown ropes and the balloon ....
4 The .... of the countryside is amazing.
5 I look for a .... place, like a big field.
6 I carefully .... the balloon on the ground.

1 Listen and read. Then number the days in order.

.... : Take a helicopter flight over New York City.

Day 1 : Fly to New York. Take off: 7 a.m. and land: 12:15 p.m.

.... : Visit the Statue of Liberty by water taxi.

.... : Morning – Go to the zoo in Central Park. Afternoon – going shopping.

.... : Visit the Empire State Building. Eat at Joe's Burger Café.

2 Listen again. Write the verbs you hear in the present progressive.

base verb	present progressive
go	I'm not going
take off	
land	
shop	
visit	
take	
climb	
eat	

3 Imagine a dialogue with Justin. Ask and answer. Use the verbs in Activity 2.

I'm not going … *What are you doing …?*
When are you …? *We're flying to …*

A: *What are you doing on Day 1?*

B: *I'm not going to school. We're going to New York.*

Grammar Central

Present progressive for future

We 're .... flying to New York tomorrow.
I'm not .... to school.
Are you .... at Joe's Café on Tuesday?

Lesson 3

Telling Stories

1 Listen and read.

2 **Ask a friend about their next vacation.**

"hanging out at home
flying to …
visiting friends
going to …"

A: What are you doing for vacation?

B: I'm hanging out at home.

3 Look at the story. Where do you think the characters are?

4 Read the story extract and answer.

1 Why does the balloon start to go down?

....

....

....

2 What do you think is going to happen to Joe?

....

....

....

3 What type of story is this? Why do you think this?

....

....

....

Lesson 4

Time to Think

1 **Read the story in your Reader.**

Why did Joe jump out of the balloon?

2 **Comprehension**

1 What was the name of the lake?

---

2 Why did Joe sleep in a tree?

---

3 What happened to the balloon when they got home?

---

4 Did Richard enjoy the balloon trip?

---

3 **Critical Literacy**

1 Where would you like to travel to in a balloon?

2 How do you think the doctor felt about the trip after Joe jumped out of the balloon?

Writing Workshop Writing captions and time expressions.

4 **Find examples of captions in the story. Write a summary of the story in captions.**

One month later, they flew to Lake Chad by balloon.

Suddenly, ...

Writing Tools

Use time expressions to link events:

Time expressions help write about events in the order that they happen.

Later, ... **Meanwhile, ...**

The next morning, ... **Suddenly, ...**

5 **Text Connections**

Where's the most exciting place you've read about?

Lesson 5

BOOK CLUB

1 Listen and read. Who were the Montgolfier brothers?

Scarlett: Well, has anyone here ever been in a hot air balloon?

Yasmin: No, but I'd love to do something exciting like that.

Rufus: Do you know anything about the Montgolfier brothers?

Yasmin: No. Who are they? I don't know anything about them.

Angelo: Yes! They invented the hot air balloon in 1783.

Yasmin: Did anyone travel in it?

Angelo: The first passengers were a sheep, a chicken, and a duck! Everyone was amazed. No one believed the flight was possible.

Yasmin: Wow! How do you know everything? What are you hiding?

Angelo: Nothing!

Yasmin: Oh, it's a book.

Angelo: Yes. Someone gave me a book about balloons.

2 Choose the best word.

someone everything anyone
something anything
no one ~~everyone~~

1 Rufus asked ..everyone........ if they knew about the Mongolfier brothers.

2 Yasmin doesn't know .... about the inventors of the hot air balloon.

3 Did .... believe the first balloon flight was possible? No, ... did.

4 Angelo was hiding .... from Yasmin.

5 Angelo knows .... about balloons. .... gave him a book.

3 Talk to a friend about the topics below. Use the indefinite pronouns in Activity 2.

"computers helicopters New York sports"

A: *I don't know anything about balloons.*

B: *I know someone who went in a balloon.*

Grammar Central

Indefinite pronouns

.....Someone...... gave me a book.

I don't know .... about the Montgolfier brothers.

Did .... travel in it?

SONG

1 **Listen and sing. Which continents is he visiting?**

I'm Going Around the World

I'm leaving tomorrow, I'm going on a trip.
I'm traveling by airplane, balloon, train, and ship.
Asia and Africa, Europe, Australia.
North and South America and Antarctica.

I'm going around the world with a compass and a map.
A tent and my passport in a heavy backpack.
I'm visiting every continent. North, south, east, and west.
Then I'm coming home because home is always best.

Everyone needs someone.
And somewhere to call their own.
For me that somewhere is here,
And this house is my home.

2 **Talk to a friend about your trip. Use the words from the song.**

A: *I'm traveling by airplane to Australia.*

B: *I'm taking my passport in my backpack.*

Spelling Central

Circle the compound nouns in the song. Compound nouns are made with two or more words.

Write the words in the chart. Can you add more compound nouns?

compound nouns	made with these words
airplane	air + plane

1 **Read. Where do the turtles lay their eggs?**

Turtle Travels

1 The Journey Begins

Every two or three years, Atlantic green turtles leave their home in Brazil in South America. They travel over 2,000 kilometers east to Ascension Island in the South Atlantic Ocean.

No one knows for sure how they find their way. They might have a kind of natural compass inside their bodies.

2 ....

The journey takes several months. The turtles don't eat anything. Some die on the way because they choke on plastic bags or fishermen catch them illegally.

3 ....

They arrive at Ascension Island. At night when it's dark, the females lay about 100 eggs on the beach. They bury them in nests in the sand. Then, the adult turtles swim back to Brazil.

4 ....

Birds and other animals eat some of the eggs. Two months later, the remaining eggs hatch. The tiny turtles try to run down the beach to the ocean. They follow the light from the moon. Many of them get lost or crabs and birds eat them. Humans also catch turtles illegally to make turtle soup or jewelry from their shells.

5 ....

The survivors find food in the water and then they swim west to join the adult turtles back in Brazil. A few years later, these survivors are going to swim back to the island where they were born.

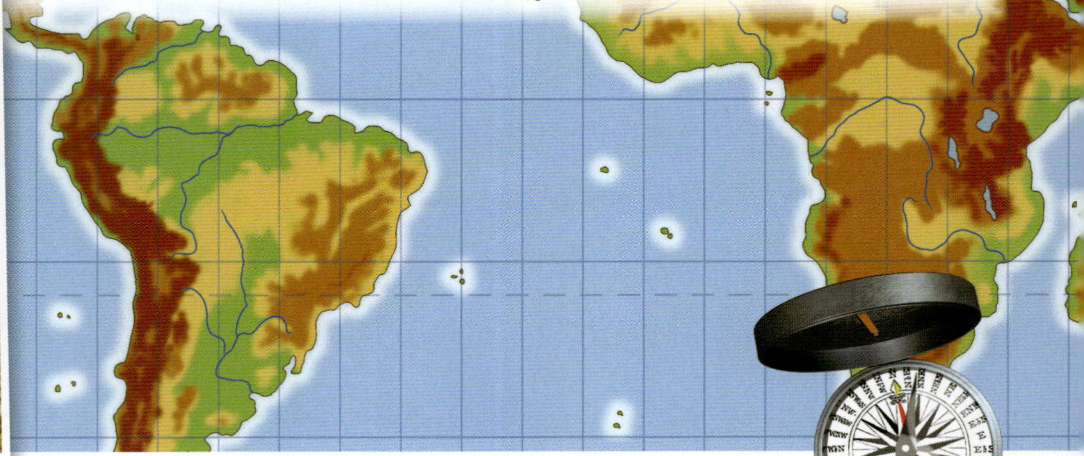

2 **Match the headings to the paragraphs.**

Nests in the Sand
Babies in Danger
~~The Journey Begins~~
Going Home
A Difficult Journey

3 **Discuss.**

Should we protect the turtles? Why? / Why not?

4 **Find Out More!**

Find out about another animal that migrates. Which direction do they travel and why?

Search Engine

When you search for factual information, use websites that are well known for that subject, e.g., for facts about animals, try a natural history museum website.

Lesson 8

Prepare

1 In groups, look at a map and plan a week-long trip.

"Let's fly south …
Why don't we go to …?
I'd like to go to …
Then let's go to …"

Write

2 **Write an itinerary for a trip.**

- Mark your route on a map.
- Write your itinerary.

  Day 1: Fly to …
  Day 2: Take boat to …
  Day 3: …

- Write a paragraph about the trip you arranged.

  Describe where and when you're going, how you're traveling, and what you're going to do when you arrive.

Writing Tools

When you write an itinerary:
Write in note form, using the simple present tense.
Use the present progressive tense and time expressions.

Showcase

3 **Present your itinerary and tell the class about your trip.**

Reflect

4 **Vote for the best trip itinerary and talk to the class.**

I liked it because they're going to interesting places.

I liked it because they're taking a tent.

Review

1 Listen and mark the route. Then complete with the correct form of the verbs.

land ~~take off~~ stop fly travel

1 They're *taking off* .... in five minutes.
2 They're .... east over the Rocky Mountains.
3 They're .... over the Great Lakes.
4 They're .... in Chicago.
5 They're .... in New York.

2 Write sentences in your notebook about the map. Use these words:

something someone anything
anyone no one nothing

Do you know anything about New York?
I know someone who has been to ...

3 Think about Chapter 4. Color the bone.

Which activity was easy? ....

Which activity was difficult? ....

Figure it out with a friend.

Write a tip to help you remember.
....
....

Treasure Hunt!

Look back at pages 4 and 5.

In which continent was *The Great Balloon Adventure*? Find Lake Chad on the map.

Find something from that continent. What is it?

Chapter 5 Real or Imaginary?

Lesson 1

1 Listen and write the prices.

1 sweater $ 25.50
2 dress $ ....
3 necklace $ ....
4 T-shirt $ ....
5 boots $ ....
6 ring $ ....
7 handbag $ ....

2 **Listen again and write the words next to the clues.**

plastic leather ~~wool~~ cotton glass silver wood silk

1 It's very soft and warm. wool
2 The cloth is so light. ....
3 It's from an apple tree. ....
4 It's nice to wear when it's hot. ....
5 It's strong and natural. ....
6 Gold is more expensive than this metal. ....
7 This is recycled from old bottles. ....
8 Your things won't get wet. ....

1 Read. Who might buy these things and why?

For Sale | sign in | search | buy

Cotton bag
Condition: new
Description: big green bag made of cotton. Can be used for shopping or for clothes.

Price: $15

New toy
Condition: new
Description: This is a new toy train. It's made of wood and has red plastic wheels.

Price: $25

Silver jewelry box
Condition: old
Description:

This little box is made of wood and is decorated with small pieces of silver. It's very old and beautiful and is used for jewelry.

Price: $18

Moroccan slippers
Condition: new
Description: These beautiful shoes are from Morocco and are made of soft leather. They're decorated with little glass beads. A lot of different colors and sizes.

Price: $20

Recycled plastic handbag
Condition: new
Description: This handbag is made of recycled plastic bags. It's orange and white. Can be used for money or pencils.

Price: $8

2 Read again and complete the chart. Then talk to a friend.

object	material	price $
bag	cotton	

A: *What's the bag made of?*
B: *It's made of cotton.*
A: *How much is it?*
B: *It's $15.*

3 Talk to a friend about your clothes and possessions.

What's your … made of?
What are your … made of?
It's made of …
They're made of …

A: *What's your shirt made of?*
B: *It's made of cotton.*

Grammar Central

be made of / used for

What's the bag made of ?
It's .... cotton.
It's .... carrying shopping.

Lesson 3
Telling Stories

1 Listen and read.

2 **Imagine you are hungry. Talk to a friend about food.**

"Those cookies …
Those cupcakes …
Those sandwiches …
This chocolate …"

A: Mm. I'm hungry. Those cookies look good.
B: Help yourself!
A: Thanks. Did you make them?
B: Yes, I did!

THIS STRANGE LAND

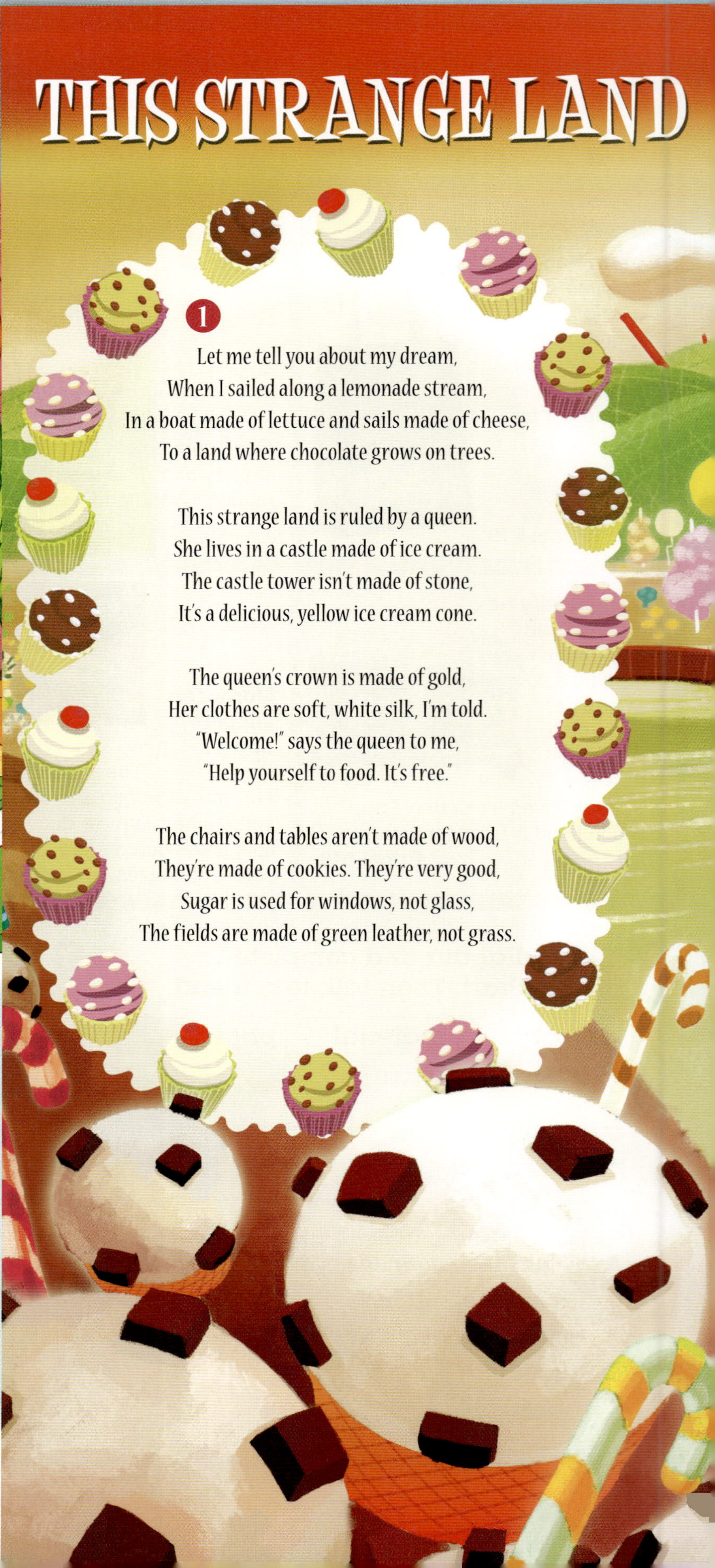

1

Let me tell you about my dream,
When I sailed along a lemonade stream,
In a boat made of lettuce and sails made of cheese,
To a land where chocolate grows on trees.

This strange land is ruled by a queen.
She lives in a castle made of ice cream.
The castle tower isn't made of stone,
It's a delicious, yellow ice cream cone.

The queen's crown is made of gold,
Her clothes are soft, white silk, I'm told.
"Welcome!" says the queen to me,
"Help yourself to food. It's free."

The chairs and tables aren't made of wood,
They're made of cookies. They're very good,
Sugar is used for windows, not glass,
The fields are made of green leather, not grass.

3 Look at the story. What do you think is strange about the land?

4 Read the story extract and answer.

1 What are the queen's clothes made of?

---

2 What do you think is going to happen to the boy on his journey?

---

3 Is the strange land real or imaginary?

Lesson 4

Time to Think

1 **Read the story in your Reader.**

How many different things are there to eat and drink?

2 **Comprehension**

1 Why did the boy want to catch chocolate fish?

2 What happens to the boat?

3 How did the boy escape from the giant fish?

4 Did you know something bad was going to happen? What were the clues?

3 **Critical Literacy**

1 Why do you think the queen was sad?

2 Would you like to visit an imaginary place like the Strange Land?

Writing Workshop Using adjectives to make your writing more interesting.

4 **Find examples of adjectives in the story and write them in the chart. Write some more descriptions for an imaginary land.**

opinion	size	shape	age	color	material	noun
delicious	small			yellow	chocolate	fish

A beautiful, small, round, red flower.

Writing Tools

Use adjectives to make your writing more interesting:

beautiful
big round
old green
silk

5 **Text Connections**

Do you know any other stories about imaginary lands?

Lesson 5

BOOK CLUB

1 Listen and read. Are there penguins in Africa?

Scarlett: The Strange Land sounds a bit scary, but amazing.

Rufus: Yes, imagine a land where chairs are made of cookies and chocolate grows on trees. Mm!

Yasmin: Hey, Angelo, true or false? 1) Chocolate grows on trees.

Angelo: It's true! Chocolate is made from cocoa, and cocoa trees are grown all over South America.

Yasmin: That's right. 2) Brazilian is spoken in Brazil.

Angelo: False. They don't speak Brazilian. They speak Portuguese.

Yasmin: Correct. 3) Kangaroos are eaten in Australia.

Angelo: True. They eat kangaroo meat in Australia.

Yasmin: That's right. 4) Penguins are found in Africa.

Angelo: No way! Penguins like cold countries.

Yasmin: No, it's true. They live in South Africa, too. 5) The moon is made of cheese.

Angelo: Now you're being silly!

Yasmin: Ha, ha, ha, ha!

2 Write passive sentences.

1 Farmers grow cocoa trees in South America.
Cocoa trees are grown in South America.

2 They speak Portuguese in Brazil.
____

3 People eat kangaroos in Australia.
____

4 You can find penguins in Africa.
____

3 Complete with the correct form of the verb. Then talk to a friend.

play grow ~~ride~~ make

1 Ostriches are (ride) ridden in South Africa.

2 Basketball is (play) ______ in India.

3 Glass is (make) ______ of sand.

4 Cotton is (grow) ______ on plants.

A: *Ostriches are ridden in South Africa.*

B: *Yes, that's true!*

Grammar Central

Present passive

Soccer ______ at my school.
Spanish and English ______ in a lot of countries.

Lesson 6

1 Listen and write the captions. Which countries eat the most chocolate?

Roast and **grind** the beans.	~~**Pick** ripe cocoa pods.~~
Deliver the beans.	**Remove** the beans.
Collect and **dry** the beans.	**Mix** the paste with sugar and milk to make chocolate.

2 Talk to a friend. Use the words from Activity 1 to talk about how chocolate is made.

A: *First, the ripe cocoa pods are picked.*

B: *Then, the beans are removed.*

Spelling Central

Use the verbs in the text. Write the past participles in the chart.

Can you add more past participles?

+ *-d*	+ *-ed*	change *-y* to *-ied*	irregular
removed	picked		

How Tempera Paint is Made

1 **Read. Number the paragraphs in order.**

An Egg-cellent Painting!

1 This is how all artists used to make their paint many years ago. These days, paint can be bought in stores, but some artists still like to make paint this way. It's called "tempera" and it's made with eggs!

☐ Some water is added to make the paint easier to use.

☐ Next, a pigment is added. Pigments give paints their color. Pigments of different colors are made from plants, precious stones, and metals. Even insects are collected, dried, and then ground to make colorful powders.

☐ Tempera paint has to be used very quickly. Can you guess why?

☐ The pigment is mixed with the egg yolk to make a paste. The paste is ground until it's very smooth.

☐ First, an egg is broken and removed from its shell. Only the yolk, the yellow part, is used to make paint, so all of the white part has to be removed. Then, the egg yolk is cleaned very carefully.

2 **Write T (true) or F (false).**

1 Egg white is used to make paint. F

2 Insects are used to give paint its color. ☐

3 The pigment can be precious stone. ☐

4 Tempera paint can be mixed with water. ☐

5 The egg shell needs to be cleaned. ☐

6 Artists used to make their paint from eggs. ☐

3 **Discuss.**

Why do you think some artists still make paint this way instead of buying it?

4 **Find Out More!**

Research one of the following: cotton, tea, coffee. Then choose another product to find out more about. How is it made?

Search Engine

Try searching for flow charts or other diagrams. They can help you understand a process more easily.

Lesson 8

PROJECT

Prepare

1 In groups, talk about a fantasy land.

There are …
There aren't any …
The land is ruled by …
The trees are made of …

Write

2 Write a poem.

- Draw a picture of your fantasy land and a creature that lives there.
- Write a verse describing the fantasy land.
- Write a verse describing a fantasy creature that lives in your land.
- Then write a verse about what happens there.

Writing Tools

When you write a poem:

Start each new line with a capital letter.
Use a comma or a period at the end of each line.
It does not have to rhyme. It should have a rhythm and sound good when read aloud.

Showcase

3 Present your poem to the class.

Reflect

4 Vote for the best poem and talk to the class.

There were a lot of strange trees.

I liked it when the girl saw the fantasy creature.

1 Listen and write sentences.

1 carpets / make / of wool ___ The carpets are made of wool.
2 carpets / make / in the villages ___
3 leather / use for / shoes ___
4 olives / grow / in the mountains ___
5 olives / deliver / to the towns ___
6 English / speak / in the markets ___

2 Write sentences in your notebook about Morocco. Use some of these words.

made spoken eaten grown
ridden ground picked

Carpets are made in Morocco.

3 Think about Chapter 5. Color the bone.

Which activity was easy? ___

Which activity was difficult? ___

Figure it out with a friend.

Write a tip to help you remember.
___
___

Treasure Hunt!

Look back at pages 4 and 5.

Where's cocoa mainly grown? Find the continent on the map.

Find something from a country on that continent.

Chapter 6 On the Ocean Waves

Lesson 1

1 Listen and check (✓) the true statements.

Museum of the Sea

Join the lifeboat crew!

1 ☐ Alice is a new lifeboat volunteer.
2 ☐ There are only men in the crew.
3 ☐ We rescue people.
4 ☐ We only go out in the lifeboat in good weather.
5 ☐ We don't wear life jackets.
6 ☐ We save lives!

2 **Listen again and write the words next to the clues.**

save	rescue	~~lifeboat~~
sinking	life jacket	drown
crew	rock	survivor

1 This is a very strong boat. lifeboat

2 To help some people in danger. ....

3 Something hard under the ocean. ....

4 A boat going down into the water. ....

5 There are 16 people in our ....

6 We wear them to keep us safe. ....

7 People .... and die in the ocean.

8 Four people didn't die. ....

9 We .... lives.

1 Read. What happened to the passengers?

Ship Hits Rocks and Sinks

Saturday, January 14th, 2012

The Concordia cruise ship hit a rock at 9:45 p.m. yesterday evening. The ship was sailing in the Mediterranean Sea along the coast of Italy when it hit a **rock**. There were more than 4,000 passengers and crew on board. They were eating their dinner when they heard a loud noise. Then the lights went off. The Concordia was sinking. Some passengers got into **lifeboats**, some had **life jackets** and swam to an island, but others **drowned**. This morning, divers were still looking for **survivors**.

2 Circle the past progressive verbs in the text, and underline the simple past verbs.

3 Make sentences for the passengers and crew.

1 sit on deck / ship sink
The passengers were sitting on deck when the ship sank.

2 get into bed / lights go off

3 serve drinks / ship hit a rock

4 eat dinner / hear a loud noise

5 look for survivors / hear somebody shout

6 swim to an island / lifeboat rescue me

4 Imagine a dialogue with a survivor. Ask and answer.

"What were you doing ...?
How did you ...?
What happened when ...?
Did you feel ...?"

A: What were you doing when the ship sank?
B: I was listening to music in my cabin.

Grammar Central

Past progressive

I ______ my homework when you walked in.
We ______ TV when the doorbell rang.

Lesson 3

Telling Stories

1 Listen and read.

2 **Imagine you are worried about something. Give your friend reassurance.**

"be late for …
miss the bus
fail the exam
find the classroom"

A: Oh, no! Are we going to miss the bus?

B: No. Don't worry. It's going to be OK.

The Journal

⑧ The passengers and crew were waiting for the captain to give orders. There were so many people, and it was very confusing.

⑫ Then, it was our turn. We were waiting in line when a man pushed in front of us. He was very frightened and was shouting. But an officer pulled him away.

STORY

(10) *No one wanted to go. I saw a lady in a green coat. She was crying and holding her baby tightly. Her husband kissed them both and said goodbye. Then, she got in the lifeboat and sat down, and they rowed away.*

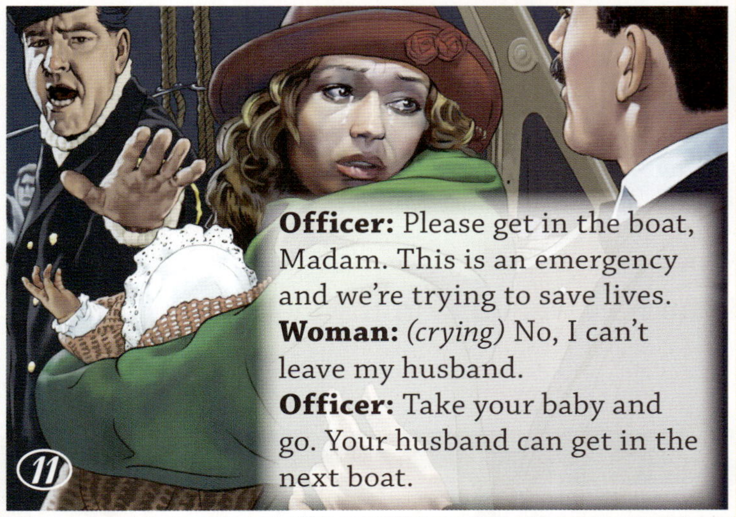

3 **Look at the story. Who do you think wrote the journal pages?**

4 **Read the story extract and answer.**

1 Why are the characters getting into a lifeboat?

....

....

....

2 What do you think is going to happen to the journal?

....

....

....

3 How are the characters dressed?

....

....

....

Lesson 4

Time to Think

1 Read the story in your Reader.

Why was the *Titanic* sinking?

2 Comprehension

1 What was Aunt Edith wearing when she got into the lifeboat?

---

2 Why was nobody running or shouting at first?

---

3 When do you think people became scared?

---

4 Why did the man want to get into the lifeboat?

---

3 Critical Literacy

1 How do you think Aunt Edith felt in this story?
2 Why do you think the women and children went first in the lifeboats?

Writing Workshop Writing a dialogue.

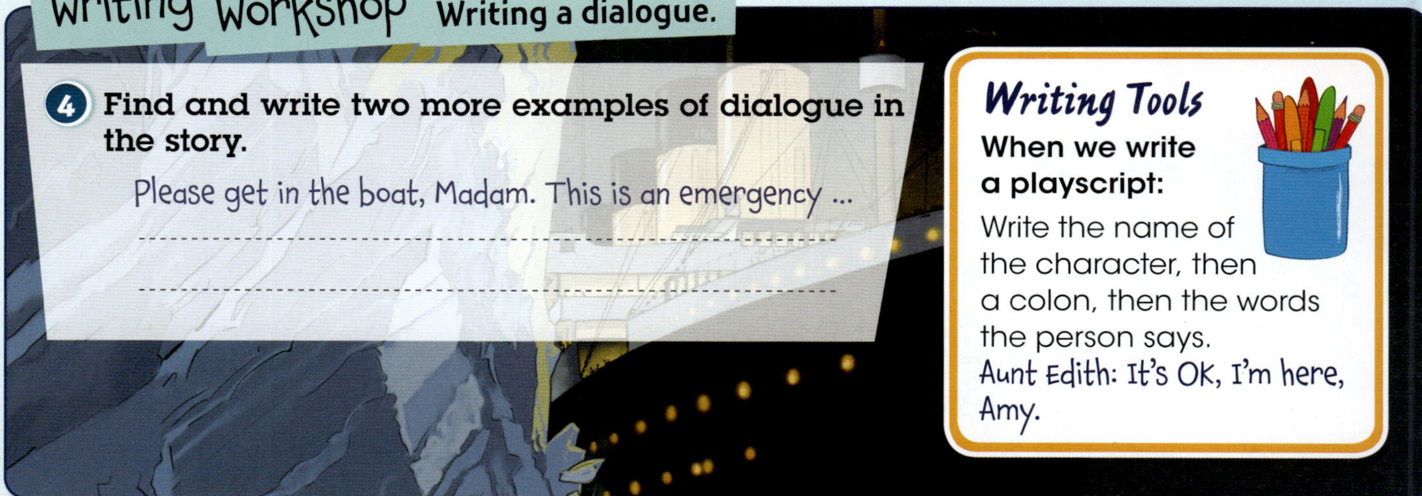

4 Find and write two more examples of dialogue in the story.

Please get in the boat, Madam. This is an emergency ...

Writing Tools

When we write a playscript:

Write the name of the character, then a colon, then the words the person says.

Aunt Edith: It's OK, I'm here, Amy.

5 Text Connections

Do you know any more information about the *Titanic*?

Lesson 5

BOOK CLUB

1 Listen and read. Why didn't Angelo know about the *Titanic*?

Scarlett: Were you listening to that story?

Rufus: Yes, I was, but while I was listening, I was looking up the *Titanic* on the Internet. Listen. Another ship, called the *Carpathia*, tried to rescue them.

Yasmin: Was the *Carpathia* close to the *Titanic* while it was sinking?

Rufus: No, it didn't arrive for almost two hours, but it picked up more than 700 survivors. A lot of the passengers on the *Titanic* were leaving England.

Yasmin: Where were they going?

Rufus: They were going to live in America. They were sailing close to Newfoundland when they saw the iceberg.

Scarlett: And was the band really still playing music while the ship was sinking?

Rufus: Well, yes, some people say it was.

Angelo: Really? I didn't know that.

Yasmin: But we just read that in the story!

Angelo: Oh, sorry. While you were reading the story, I fell asleep.

2 Write *when* or *while*.

1 What was Rufus doing ___while___ he was listening to the story?

2 Where were the passengers going ______ the ship sank?

3 Where was the ship sailing to ______ they saw the iceberg?

4 What was the band doing ______ the ship was sinking?

5 What was Yasmin doing ______ Angelo fell asleep?

3 Ask and answer the questions in Activity 2.

A: *What was the band doing while the ship was sinking?*

B: *It was playing music.*

Grammar Central

Past progressive: *when / while*

___While___ you were reading the story, I fell asleep.

When I fell asleep you were ______ the story.

What ______ you doing while the ship was sinking?

Lesson 6

SONG

1 **Listen and order the pictures. What did the cabin boy do and why?**

The Golden Vanity

A ship sailed out on the Lowland Sea.
The ship's name was the Golden Vanity.
The captain, crew, and cabin boy,
Were sleeping when they heard, "Ship ahoy!"
Yo, ho, ho! Away we go! Sailing out on the ocean waves!

A big black flag was flying from the mast.
The pirate ship was approaching fast!
"Destroy them!" said the captain to the boy.
"Sink their ship and this gold is yours."

The pirates were busy eating their meal,
When the boy dived into the icy sea.
He made three holes in the side of their boat.
The boat was sinking. Now it couldn't float!

"Hooray!" said the men on the Golden Vanity.
As they pulled the boy from the icy sea.
"We can all go home to our children and wives.
Thanks to the cabin boy for saving our lives."

2 **Talk to a friend about the *Golden Vanity*. Use the words from the song.**

A: *The ship was sailing on the Lowland Sea when the crew saw a pirate ship.*

Spelling Central

Circle the irregular plurals in the song. Write the words in the chart. Can you add any more irregular plurals?

singular	plural
man	men

1 Read. What is a good thing and what is a bad thing about icebergs?

What are Icebergs?

Icebergs are floating islands made of ice. Most are found in the North Atlantic Ocean and Antarctica. They're very dangerous for ships. An iceberg can be as small as a car or as big as a country like Jamaica. Even small icebergs are very heavy and can destroy a ship, or make a big hole in it. Only about 15% of an iceberg can be seen above the water. Most of it is below the ocean. Since the *Titanic* sank, the position of icebergs is now shown on maps and the North Atlantic Ocean is much safer for ships.

An iceberg is made of snow so it is fresh water, not salt water like the ocean. The ice melts and makes pools of water on top of the iceberg, and birds and other creatures can drink this. Some animals and birds, like polar bears, penguins, and seals, make their homes on and around icebergs.

When they float toward warmer water, icebergs start to melt. The planet is getting warmer so more icebergs are melting.

2 Write T (true) or F (false).

1 Icebergs can destroy ships. T

2 Most of the iceberg is above the water. ☐

3 Icebergs are shown on maps. ☐

4 Icebergs are made of salt water. ☐

5 Some animals live on icebergs. ☐

6 Icebergs melt when the water is very cold. ☐

3 Discuss.

Did we learn anything from the *Titanic* disaster? Yes or no?

4 Find Out More!

What does global warming mean? What happens to sea levels?

Search Engine

When you search for factual information, compare different websites and books to make sure the facts are correct.

Prepare

1 In groups, imagine you were on the *Titanic*. Talk about what happened.

"I was sleeping when …
I felt frightened when …
There was a loud noise …
While I was eating dinner, …"

Write

2 Write a diary entry.

- Write some notes about what happened when the *Titanic* sank.

  Where was the *Titanic* going?
  What year and day was it?
  Who was traveling on the *Titanic*?
  What happened that day?

- Imagine you were on the *Titanic*. Write a diary entry.

Writing Tools

When you write a diary entry:
Write the day and the date at the top.
Write about the events in the order that they happened.

Story Central Level 5 Chapter 6 Lesson 8

1912

TITANIC SINKS

WHITE STAR LINE
Traveling from: Southampton
Traveling to: New York City
On (date): April 10th On (ship): Titanic
Passenger name: Juan

1912

Day: Monday Date: April 15th

Dear Diary:
Today was a terrible day. I was sleeping in my bed when I heard a noise. I didn't want to get up. It was cold outside. Somebody knocked on the door. They told me to go to the deck. While I was getting dressed. I heard people shouting. I ran to the deck and I saw an iceberg. I was frightened when I saw it because it was so big. We got into the lifeboat while the band was still playing.

Showcase

3 Present your diary entry to the class.

Reflect

4 Vote for the best diary entry and talk to the class.

"I liked it because it was realistic."

"I liked it when she saw the iceberg."

1 Listen and complete with the correct form of the verbs.

1 They (sail) ......were sailing...... around the world when the accident (happen) ......happened.......

2 While they (sleep) .... the whales (hit) .... the boat.

3 Their sailing boat (sink) .... while they (watch) .... it.

4 They (have to) .... catch fish when they had no more food.

5 While they (fish) .... one day, their fishing pole (break) ....

6 They (see) .... sharks while they (float) .... across the ocean.

7 At last, the crew of a boat (see) .... them and (rescue) .... them.

2 Write sentences in your notebook about Bill and Simone. Imagine their recount of the story.

We were sailing ...
I was sleeping when ...
We jumped ...
After 20 days, we had to ...

3 Think about Chapter 6. Color the bone.

Treasure Hunt!

Look back at pages 4 and 5.

Where did the *Titanic* sink? Find the place on the map.

Find something from that ocean. What is it?

Chapter 7 Let's Cook!

Lesson 1

1 Listen and write the quantities.

Vegetable Soup Recipe

Ingredients

2 onions
..... tomatoes
..... potato
..... cabbage
..... carrots
..... spoon of oil
a little salt and pepper

2 Listen again and write the missing words.

oil chop fry boil pan pepper pour ~~slice~~

1 Slice the cabbage.
2 ..... the other vegetables.
3 ..... the onions in hot .....
4 Put the other vegetables in the .....
5 ..... some water and ..... it over the vegetables.
6 Add a little salt and .....

1 Read. Write a name for the recipe.

_________________ **recipe**

1 First, chop the chicken into pieces.
2 Then, pour some oil into a pan. When it's hot, add the chicken carefully.
3 Fry the chicken slowly until it is brown.
4 Meanwhile, wash the lettuce well. Slice the tomatoes and cucumber thinly and make a salad.
5 Put the chicken on top of the salad.
6 Mix some oil and lemon juice quickly. Add a little salt and pepper.
7 Pour it over the salad and eat immediately.

2 Find the adverbs in the text. Write the adverbs and adjectives in the chart.

adverb	adjective
carefully	careful

Grammar Central

Adverbs

That's very noisy. Can you do that ____________, please?
I did really ____________ on the exam. I couldn't answer anything.

3 Choose a verb and an adverb. Give instructions to a friend.

slice pour fry chop

carefully quickly loudly angrily

A: *Slice the bread carefully …*

Lesson 3

Telling Stories

1 Listen and read.

2 Talk to a friend about things you have done.

> cook dinner
> write a poem
> run a kilometer
> make a cake

A: *I cooked dinner last night.*

B: *Anyone can cook dinner. It's easy!*

The Best Food in the World

"Rashmi, come quickly! Your brothers are coming home today. Clean the house."

Rashmi is cleaning.

Her mother sits by the door patiently. "They're here!" she shouts suddenly.

Rashmi looks up and sees two men, dressed well.

"Maa!" shout the men, dropping their luggage and greeting their mother.

"Rashmi, you've grown!" says Kuntal.

Mrs. Kapoor is in the village talking to her neighbor. "My older son, Kuntal, is a chef in the best restaurant in New York. He cooks so well! *And* Shabar makes beautiful cakes for the best bakery in Paris. So smart!
We haven't seen them since Rashmi was little. And, they're cooking for us tonight. Can you imagine it? Two famous chefs in *my* kitchen!"

Later...
"Don't get in the way, Rashmi," says Kuntal.
"Sorry, I'm just making ..."
"We're cooking dinner!" says Shabar.

STORY

3 Look at the story. Where do you think this story is set?

4 Read the story extract and answer.

1 Why is Mrs. Kapoor excited?

---

2 What do you think her sons are going to cook?

---

3 What type of food do you think Mrs. Kapoor usually cooks?

Lesson 4

Time to Think

1 **Read the story in your Reader.**

What does Kuntal cook for the family?

2 **Comprehension**

1 How do you know Maa loves her family?

2 What does Shabar's dessert look like?

3 What ingredients are in Rashmi's pudding?

4 Why do they like Rashmi's pudding?

3 **Critical Literacy**

1 Did Maa and Rashmi like Kuntal and Shabar's cooking?

2 Who do you think is the best cook?

Writing Workshop Using adverbs of manner.

4 **Find the adverbs in the story. Use the adverbs to write your own sentences.**

I walked <u>quickly</u> because I was late.

Writing Tools

Use adverbs to describe how people do things:

She's waiting patiently.

slowly carefully

well immediately

5 **Text Connections**

Do you know any other kinds of books or stories about food or cooking?

Lesson 5

1 Listen and read. Which types of food are healthy or bad for you?

Yasmin: That story made me hungry! What are you eating?

Angelo: Potato chips. Have some.

Yasmin: OK, just one, thanks. There's too much salt on them! You shouldn't eat too many chips you know, Angelo. Salt is bad for you. Most people eat too much salt and sugar in their food. Did you know there are ten teaspoons of sugar in a can of cola? That's so bad for your teeth! And most people in the Western world don't eat enough fruit and vegetables. You know, you should have five or more pieces of fruit or vegetables every day. Some people eat none!

Angelo: Potatoes are vegetables.

Yasmin: Yes, but I'm talking about green vegetables. And chips are fried so they have too much fat, too. A small bag of chips has about two and a half teaspoons of oil in it.

Angelo: Can I have mine back then?

Yasmin: Oh! I ate them all! Sorry!

2 Complete with the correct quantifiers.

too much
too many enough

1 Angelo eats five teaspoons of salt a day. He eats too much salt.

2 Some children drink cola every day. That's ________ sugar.

3 Some people eat one piece of fruit every day. They don't eat ________ fruit.

4 Angelo likes potatoes but he doesn't eat ________ green vegetables.

5 Yasmin ate all the potato chips. She ate ________ potato chips.

3 Write your answers. Then talk to a friend about what you eat.

1 How many pieces of fruit and vegetables do you eat every day? ________

2 Do you eat potato chips every day? ________

3 How many times a week do you drink cola? ________

A: *I eat three or four pieces of fruit every day.*

B: *That's OK, but you don't eat enough vegetables.*

Grammar Central

Quantifiers: *too much / too many / enough*

I eat too many cookies and I drink ________ cola.

I don't drink ________ water and I don't eat ________ fruit.

Lesson 6

1 **Listen and check (✓). Which food does the boy give the girl?**

2 **Listen again and write the words from Activity 1.**

1 It's **juicy**, and **tastes** sweet and a little bit **sour**. tomato

2 It's **soft** and **sweet** and **tasty**. It tastes like a pear. ....

3 It's **bitter**. ....

4 It's **crunchy** and **salty**. ....

5 It's **smelly**. It **smells** like a lemon. ....

3 **Talk to a friend about food. Use the words in Activity 2.**

A: *Do you like tomatoes?*

B: *No, I don't. They're too sour.*

Spelling Central

Circle the words that end with -*y*. These adjectives are formed by adding -*y* to other words.

Can you add more adjectives that end in -*y*? What happens to the words that end in -*e*?

adjectives	other word
crunchy	crunch

1 Read. Is Heston Blumenthal a chef or an artist?

Food and the Senses

Some chefs don't make tasty food just to fill your stomach. They make food that makes people think. Heston Blumenthal does this, and he made this food. It's beautiful! Some people think his food is art. Eating in his restaurant is more like going to the theater than going out for a meal. What do you think? Is it art or cooking?

This box looks and smells like a forest on a damp day. You don't eat this "forest" but you see and smell it while you're eating. This makes you taste the forest at the same time. When you see and smell, it plays with your taste buds and your brain! This isn't a new idea. In Medieval times, life was very hard, so rich people asked their chefs to make their food more fun, for entertainment.

This dish is called "Sound of the Sea." It's made of seafood and seaweed. You can eat the sand, too! The meal looks like a beach on a plate. It's very realistic. There's an MP3 player in the shell. You can listen to the ocean while you're eating. Do you think this makes the food taste different?

2 Write T (true) or F (false).

1 Heston Blumenthal has a restaurant. T
2 He works in a theater.
3 You can eat the forest.
4 Food as entertainment isn't a new idea.
5 You can't eat "Sound of the Sea."
6 There's music in the shell.

3 Discuss.

When you're eating, which sense is more important? Seeing, smelling, tasting, or feeling?

4 Find Out More!

How do your other senses change how things taste? Why do things taste different when you have a cold?

Search Engine

A question or sentence sometimes gives better search results, e.g., "taste" might give too many results. Try "Does smell change how food tastes?"

PROJECT Lesson 8

Prepare

1 **In groups, think of a dish you'd like to make and talk about the recipe.**

Let's make …
You need …
First, you chop …
Then, you …

Write

2 **Write a recipe.**

- Draw a picture and write the name of the dish.
- Write a list of ingredients. How much do you need of each food?
- Write your recipe.

Writing Tools

When you write instructions, use the imperative form of the verb:

Write instructions in order, using numbers and sequencing words.

Use adverbs to explain how things should be done.

Showcase

3 **Present your recipe to the class.**

Reflect

4 **Vote for the best recipe.**

I liked this recipe because it looked amazing.

The ingredients were tasty.

1 Listen and circle the words. Then number the sentences in order.

- [ ] When the onion is soft, add the rice to the pan and mix *good* / *well*.
- [ ] *Boil* / *Chop* the water.
- [1] *Chop* / *Pour* the onion.
- [ ] *Pour* / *Slice* some oil into a pan.
- [ ] The cheese is *salty* / *juicy* so don't add too *much* / *many* salt! Eat immediately! It's *tasty* / *bitter*!
- [ ] Fry the onion *slowly* / *slow*. It *smells* / *tastes* good.
- [ ] Pour the hot water *carefully* / *careful* into the pan. The rice shouldn't be *soft* / *crunchy*.

2 Write sentences in your notebook about the picture. Use these words.

salt sugar fruit vegetables

She doesn't have enough …
She eats too much …
There are too many …

3 Think about Chapter 7. Color the bone.

Which activity was easy?

Which activity was difficult?

Figure it out with a friend.

Write a tip to help you remember.

Treasure Hunt!

Look back at pages 4 and 5.

Where's the story *The Best Food in the World* set? Find the country on the map.

Find something from that country. What is it?

Chapter 8 Speak Out!

Lesson 1

1 Listen and check (✔) the rules that you hear on the poster.

Rules for a Happy Home!

1 Don't argue with your brothers and sisters. ✔
2 RESPECT your parents! ☐
3 Don't lie, tell the truth. ★★★ ☐
4 Offer to help with the chores. ☐
5 SHARE YOUR CANDY. ☐
6 ALWAYS SAY PLEASE AND THANK YOU. ☐
7 Laugh at each other's jokes. ☐
8 Say sorry. ☐
9 Agree to disagree sometimes. ☐
10 SAY "I LOVE YOU," EVERY DAY! ☐

2 Listen again and write the correct form of the missing verbs.

argue respect agree disagree share laugh ~~decide~~ tell offer joke lie

1 I've ___decided___ we need some rules.

2 I don't ________. Yes, you do!

3 You should ________ your parents.

4 I didn't ________. I always ________ the truth.

5 You have to ________ to help with the chores and always ________ your candy.

6 I was ________. You should ________ at my jokes!

7 Should we ________ to ________?

Lesson 2

1 **Read. Which lessons did the President go to?**

Hey, Sabine

Sorry you're sick. You missed a great day.

The President visited our school today. She told us that she spoke five languages but she didn't like traveling. She offered to help Ryan in the classroom, then joked that she couldn't do math.

After morning classes, she decided to eat with us so she could see what we had for lunch. She said our lunches were very healthy!

Then in the afternoon, she joined in a game of hockey with us. She explained that she wasn't very good at sports but we argued that she was very good at running. She was cool!

See you at school tomorrow.

Love,

Jess

2 **Write examples of reported speech from the email. Then write the direct speech.**

1 She told us that *she spoke five languages.*
"I speak five languages."

2 She said our lunches ______.
______

3 She explained that she ______.
______

4 We argued ______.
______

3 **Play "The Whispering Game" in groups of six.**

> *She said she …*
> *He told me that he …*
> *He explained that she …*
> *She said that he …*

A: *(whispers) I like ice cream.*

B: *She said she liked to scream!*

A: *Ha, ha! No, I didn't! I told you I liked ice cream!*

Grammar Central

Reported speech

"I'm very happy." – She said (that) she ______ very happy.

"I don't like traveling." – She explained (that) she ______ traveling.

Lesson 3

Telling Stories

1 Listen and read.

2 **Ask a friend for the meaning of other words in English.**

A: *How do you say "adiós" in English?*

B: *It's "goodbye."*

A: *Sorry. What did you say?*

B: *I said it was "goodbye."*

GULLIVER IN LILLIPUT

1 My name is Lemuel Gulliver.

I used to be a doctor on a ship, but one day there was a terrible storm. Our ship hit some rocks and sank. The crew drowned. I was alone. So I swam. I swam until I reached an island, where I crawled onto the beach and fell asleep.

3 Later, while I was sleeping, they moved me to a temple and chained me to the wall. The emperor came to see me, but I couldn't understand him. I pointed to my mouth. He understood and asked his men to bring food.

2 When I woke up, I heard noises. But I couldn't move. My arms and legs were tied to the ground with ropes. Then something climbed up my leg – a tiny man! Suddenly, forty more men appeared on my chest. I shouted loudly and pulled one hand free, but someone shouted "Tolgo phonac!" I didn't know what it meant, but hundreds of tiny arrows flew at me. So I decided to lie still.

4 I stayed in Lilliput for nine months. Six hundred people took care of me. They made me clothes, shared their food, and taught me their language. At first they were afraid of me, but when I could speak well, they asked where I came from. I answered that I was from England, but they only knew Lilliput and Blefuscu, a nearby island. They joked that they thought I fell from the stars. I laughed!

STORY

3 Look at the story. When do you think this story takes place?

4 Read the story extract and answer.

1 What did Gulliver hear someone shout?

---

2 What do you think is going to happen to Gulliver in Lilliput?

---

3 Do you think the people of Lilliput are real?

Lesson 4

Time to Think

1 **Read the story in your Reader.**

What did Gulliver do in Lilliput?

---

2 **Comprehension**

1 Why did they tie him to the ground?

2 How did Gulliver communicate with the people from Lilliput?

3 When did they set him free?

4 Why did he want to escape to Blefuscu?

3 **Critical Literacy**

1 What do you think the people from Lilliput thought about Gulliver?

2 Have you ever told a true story that nobody believed?

Writing Workshop Writing reported speech.

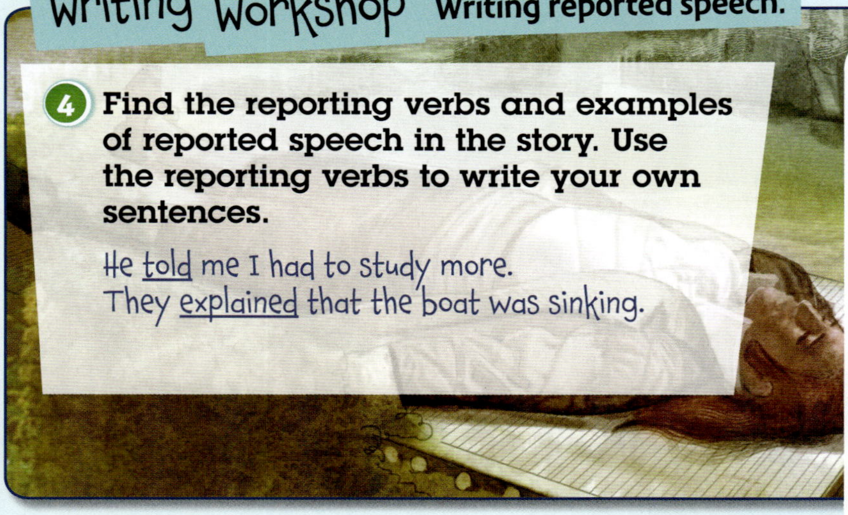

4 **Find the reporting verbs and examples of reported speech in the story. Use the reporting verbs to write your own sentences.**

He told me I had to study more.
They explained that the boat was sinking.

Writing Tools

When you write reported speech:

You don't need to use quotation marks.

They asked me where I came from.

We use quotation marks to show direct speech. This is the exact words the person used.

"I told you my story, but you didn't believe me," said Gulliver.

5 **Text Connections**

Do you know any other stories or movies from *Gulliver's Travels*?

Lesson 5

BOOK CLUB

1 Listen and read. Who did Rufus meet last summer?

Rufus: Jonathan Swift wrote *Gulliver's Travels*. It's one of my favorite books.

Yasmin: It was a great story. I'd like to meet him.

Rufus: He died in 1745.

Yasmin: Oh!

Scarlett: We met an author once.

Angelo: Really?

Rufus: Yes, she visited Story Central last summer. I asked her which books she liked and where she got her ideas.

Scarlett: That's right. I asked her what she did in her spare time.

Rufus: Oh, yes, then she asked me if I liked reading and I said I did. She asked me who my favorite author was and I said it was her. She laughed and asked me why, and I said she was the only author I've met!

Angelo: Ha, ha! That's so funny. I want to meet an author!

2 Write the questions.

1 Which books do you like?
I asked her which books she liked.
2 Where do you get your ideas?
I asked ______________
3 What do you do in your spare time?
____
4 Do you like reading?
____
5 Who's your favorite author?
____

3 Ask a friend about their reading habits. Then tell another friend.

"Do you like reading?
What's your favorite book?
Which characters do you like?
Do you read in bed?"

A: *Do you like reading?*
B: *Ana asked me if I liked reading.*

Grammar Central

Reported speech: questions

direct speech	reported speech
"Where do you live?"	He asked where I ______.
"Do you like reading?"	She asked if I ______ reading.

Lesson 6

SONG

1 Listen and sing. Which language can everyone understand?

I Don't Understand!

Can you **repeat** that?
What did you say?
What language are you speaking?
Can you **translate**?

You have a nice **accent**.
But I don't **understand**.
Take time, **pronounce** it clearly.
Can you use your hands?

Grammar is very difficult,
Vocabulary, too.
Use **signs** and **body language**,
To help me understand you.

Aah! Now it makes sense.
I know what you **mean**.
In all the different languages,
To **smile** means the same!

2 Talk to a friend. Do these speaking activities.

1 Repeat this five times:

> "Red leather, yellow leather, red leather, yellow leather."

2 Translate "body language" into your language.
3 Say something in a funny accent.
4 Make a sign for "sunny".
5 Pronounce "communication" correctly.
6 Smile. Is your friend smiling, too?

Spelling Central

Circle the words in the song that end in *–e*. Can you hear this letter? How do you pronounce this?

Write the words in the chart. Can you add more words that end in *–e*?

words ending in silent *–e*
language

World Language Statistics

1 **Read. When is it easier to learn a language?**

Languages Around the World

More than six thousand languages are spoken in the world today. More people speak Mandarin Chinese than any other language. English is the second most spoken language, *but* English is spoken in more countries than Mandarin. 14% of people speak Mandarin Chinese as their first language, and 6% speak English as their first language.

A total of about 25% of people in the world speak English. That means a lot of these people have learned English as a second language, just like you! (People are learning new languages every day, so the numbers are always changing!)

Spanish is the third most spoken language in the world. It's the most important language in about 20 countries. (How many countries can you think of where Spanish is spoken?)

It's fun to be able to speak the language when you travel to a different country, or to communicate with people visiting your country. It's much easier to learn a new language when you are young than when you are an adult, so enjoy your language class now!

Look at this picture. It shows the top ten languages spoken in the world. Can you guess how many people speak them?

2 **Number the top three languages in order on the diagram.**

3 **Discuss.**

Is it important to learn other languages? Why? / Why not?

4 **Find Out More!**

Find out about your language. Where's it spoken? What other languages are spoken in your country?

Search Engine

For information on numbers (statistics), try searching images as well as text. Numbers shown as a graph, pie-chart, or infographic are sometimes clearer.

PROJECT

Lesson 8

Prepare

1 In groups, choose a famous person. Talk about questions you'd like to ask them.

> *Do you like …?*
> *What's your favorite …?*
> *Where do you live?*
> *Do you have any …?*

Write

2 **Write an interview report.**

- Write some interview questions.
- In pairs, act out the interview with the famous person.

A: *What's your favorite color?*
B: *My favorite color is purple.*

- Write a report of your interview.

My Interview With …
Adele

My Questions
1 What's your real name?
2 What's your favorite color?
3 What sports do you like?
4 What kind of food do you like?
5 Do you have any pets?

Caption:

The Interview
My Interview with Adele.
I asked Adele what her real name was. She said it was Adele Laurie Blue Adkins. I asked her what her favorite color was. She answered that she liked purple and pink. I asked her if she liked sports. She said that she swam and went trekking. She told me she liked Japanese food. I explained that I have a dog, and asked is she had any pets. She argued that cats were better!

"I like Japanese food"

Writing Tools

When you write an interview:
Use different reporting verbs, e.g., *asked, said, told us, answered, argued, explained*.
Only use quotation marks if you repeat the exact words spoken by your famous person.

Showcase

3 Act out your interview with a friend. Then, present your report to the class.

Reflect

4 Vote for the best report and talk to the class.

> I would like to interview her, too. The interview sounded really interesting.

> I liked it when she said she didn't know the answer.

1 Listen and complete with the correct form of the verbs.

1 She said she (speak) didn't speak English very well.
2 She explained that she (understand) ______ everything.
3 She argued that she (have) ______ a bad accent.
4 She (say) ______ that she (can) ______ pronounce vocabulary words.
5 She asked me which book I (use) ______.
6 She asked me if I (can) ______ help her with her grammar.

2 Write sentences in your notebook about the picture. Imagine you met this person. What did you ask? What did he reply?

I asked him why …
I asked him if …
He told me …

3 Think about Chapter 8. Color the bone.

Which activity was easy? ______

Which activity was difficult? ______

Figure it out with a friend.

Write a tip to help you remember.
______
______

Treasure Hunt!

Look back at pages 4 and 5.

Where's the largest country that Mandarin is spoken in? Find the country on the map.

Find something from that country. What is it?

Chapter 9 Into the Future

Lesson 1

1 Listen and check (✔) the things that are in this eco town.

buildings	☐	trees	☐
pollution	☐	trams	☐
houses	☐	bike paths	☐
cars	☐	sidewalks	☐

2 Listen again and write the words below the clues.

~~building~~ village sidewalk
bike path wildlife traffic
area tram downtown pollution

1 A shop, a house or an office.
building

2 It's the center of the city.
____

3 It's a part of a town.
____

4 Plants and birds are ______________________.

5 This is dirty air.
____

6 This is a small town.
____

7 Cars, buses, trucks, etc.
____

8 This is like an electric bus.
____

9 It's a small road for bikes.
____

10 This is a road for people to walk on.
____

Lesson 2

1 Listen and read. Which town do you think should win the competition?

Competition Entry A

My town will be on a big island in the sea. Everyone will live on smaller islands around the town. Boats will bring people to the town. Downtown there'll be a business area with stores and offices in tall buildings. There won't be any traffic because you won't need a car. There will be electric trams and moving sidewalks. People will be able to sit and enjoy the wildlife in a big park. Children won't have to go to school, they will learn at home using their computers.

Competition Entry B

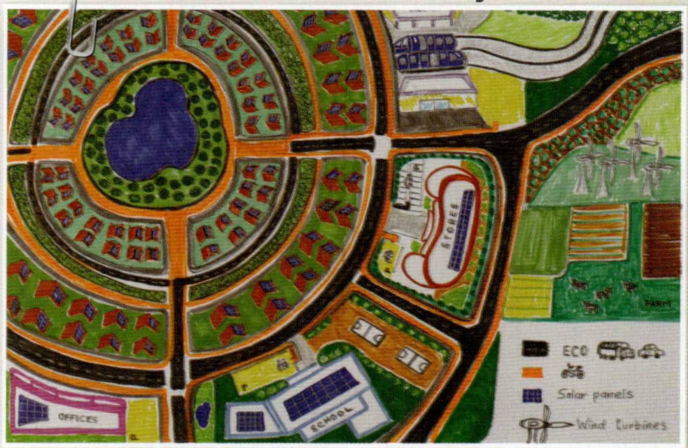

There won't be any tall buildings in my eco town, so you'll be able to see the sky. The stores won't be above the ground; they'll be under the ground. The offices will be there, too. Families will live in beautiful new houses downtown with swimming pools in the yards. The school building will be made of glass so the children can look outside. You'll be able to ride bikes around the entire town on bike paths. There won't be any other type of transportation. It will be very green.

2 Write the letter of the town.

1 There won't be a school. A
2 People will live downtown. ___
3 There won't be any tall buildings. ___
4 There will be moving sidewalks. ___
5 Children will have to go to school. ___
6 People will ride bikes everywhere. ___
7 You will be able to see a lot of wildlife. ___

3 Talk to a friend. Imagine a future town.

"There will / won't be … You will / won't … People will / won't … Children will / won't …"

A: *In my future town there will be flying cars.*
B: *You won't be able to drive in my town.*

Grammar Central

Future: *will / won't*

In the future …
everyone ______________ travel by bike or tram.
you ______________ need a car.

Lesson 3

Telling Stories

1 Listen and read.

The Memory Bank

2 **Imagine your friend has an important event tomorrow. Wish them luck.**

"the test the exam the show the soccer game"

A: What's the matter, Sophia?
B: I'm worried about the soccer game tomorrow.
A: Good luck! I'm sure you'll win!

3 **Look at the story. When do you think the story takes place?**

4 **Read the story extract and answer.**

1 Why does Dax need to visit the Memory Bank?

----

2 What do you think will happen to Dax later?

----

3 Do think the computer chip can really save memories?

Lesson 4

Time to Think

1 Read the story in your Reader.

Why is the place called the Memory Bank?

2 Comprehension

1 What is Dr. Munro's job?

2 What grade did Dax get in his exam?

3 How did Mia get some of Dax's memories?

4 Does the story have a happy ending?

3 Critical Literacy

1 Is Mia cheating if she uses Dax's memories to do her space exam?

2 Is Dax the same kind of person throughout the story or does he change?

Writing Workshop Using relative clauses to give more information.

4 Find information about these people, places, and things. Write your own relative clauses.

Mia – *the girl who hurt her head*
The memory bank – *the place where ...*
The computer chip – *the chip that ...*
your friend –
your playground –
your Story Central book –

Writing Tools

Use relative clauses to add more information to a sentence:

who **where** that

5 Text Connections

Does this story remind you of another time when technology went wrong?

Lesson 5

BOOK CLUB

1 Listen and read. Does Rufus think life will be better or worse in the future?

Rufus: That was great! I love sci-fi.

Scarlett: So what do you think? What will life be like in the future? Will people be able to store their memories?

Yasmin: Yes, I think there will be smaller computers, so it'll be easy to store a lot of information.

Rufus: In my opinion, we won't need paper anymore. And we'll just talk to our computers, so we won't need to type. It'll be great!

Scarlett: How will we travel? Will there still be cars?

Angelo: Yes, but maybe they won't use gas. They might be electric and fly.

Scarlett: And where will we live?

Rufus: We'll have to live under the ground to save energy. It's nice and warm under the ground.

Scarlett: Yasmin, why have you got a memory stick in your ear?

Yasmin: We've got a test tomorrow! I think I'll get an A+!

2 Write questions about the future.

1 What / people / wear What will people wear?
2 Where / we / live ______
3 What / children / learn / in schools ______
4 How / we / travel ______
5 What / computers / be like ______

3 Talk to a friend about the future. Use the questions in Activity 2.

A: *What will people wear?*

B: *They'll wear watches that are tiny computers.*

Grammar Central

Future: *will* questions

Will we drive cars?
Yes, we ______. / No, we ______.
What ______ people wear?

Lesson 6

1 **Listen to Sam and Jemima talking about their predictions. Write S (Sam) and J (Jemima).**

Who thinks...

1 he/she will be a vet? ....
2 electric cars will have **rechargeable batteries**? ....
3 there will be more **wind turbines**? ....
4 he/she will make **gadgets**? ....
5 everything will have **touch screen controls**? ....
6 everyone will have **solar panels** on their houses? ....
7 he/she will get married? ....
8 everything will be **wireless**? ....
9 buses will be **driverless**? ....
10 everything will be **recyclable**? ....

2 **Talk to a friend about your predictions. Use the words in Activity 1.**

A: *Do you think you will have a car?*

B: *Yes, I do. I think I'll have a car with solar panels.*

Spelling Central

Suffixes

Circle the words that end with *-able* and *-less*. What do you think these suffixes mean?

Write the words in the chart. Can you add more suffixes?

-able	*-less*
rechargeable	wireless

1 **Read and number the pictures.**

Living Tomorrow Project in Brussels

Living Tomorrow is a project about houses in the future. We've all seen wind turbines and solar panels, but some of these gadgets are like science fiction!

1 You won't need a key to get into your house. There's a fingerprint reader that opens the door. It's called a biometric entry system.

2 In the kitchen there will be a digital whiteboard that will link to every room in the house. It has touch screen controls. Each room can be made hotter or cooler using the temperature control. There's a digital shopping list linked to your refrigerator, and there's a screen to show you how much electricity and rainwater you have used.

3 In the bathroom there are intelligent mirrors. These have screens so you can check the news while you're washing your face. You can check your health too with a wireless, electric toothbrush. It shows you the results on the mirror.

4 In the children's bedroom the bed is called a "cocoon." It's like a little room with lights and a TV screen. It's really cool, but your mom can turn your TV off from the controls outside. Well, not everything in the future will be perfect!

2 **Discuss.**

Should we have more technology in the home? Why? / Why not?

3 **Find Out More!**

What will people want in their homes in the future to make their lives easier, better, or more fun?

Search Engine

Technology changes everyday so information in books and even on the Internet becomes old very quickly. Check when it was written.

PROJECT

Lesson 8

Prepare

1 **In groups, talk about what school will be like in the future.**

"I think that children will travel …
We might wear / eat / play …
I don't think children will …
We will be able to …"

Write

2 **Write about a school in the future.**
- Draw a picture of your school in the future.
- Write a paragraph about it.
- What will or won't be there?

Writing Tools

When you write about your predictions for the future:

Use *will* and *won't*
Give opinions using *I think …*
In my opinion … I believe …

Showcase

3 **Present your school to the class.**

Reflect

4 **Vote for the best description of a future school.**

I like Tom's description because he thinks there will be robots instead of teachers.

Ali believes we will have touch screens on our desks.

1 **Listen and correct the sentences.**

1 They will travel to Mars by airplane. They will travel to Mars by rocket.
2 The journey will take six months. ....
3 People on Earth won't be able to see the rocket land. ....
4 It will be very hot. ....
5 There will be a lot of food on Mars. ....
6 They will be able to come back to Earth. ....

2 **Write sentences in your notebook about the picture. Use these words.**

buildings	bike path	traffic	pollution
gadgets	driverless	electric	touch screen

I think people will ...
I don't think there will be ...
We won't be able to ...

3 **Think about Chapter 9. Color the bone.**

Which activity was easy? ....

Which activity was difficult? ....

Figure it out with a friend.

Write a tip to help you remember.
....
....

Treasure Hunt!

Look back at pages 4 and 5.

Where's the *Living Tomorrow* project in Lesson 7? Find the city on the map.

Find something from that country.

Grammar Reference

Chapter 1 Grammar

They **studied** reading, writing, and math.
The boys and girls **had to** sit separately.
Did the girls **wear** dresses? Yes, they **did.**
Did the boys **wear** pants? No, they **didn't.**

Circle the correct option.
We use the simple past tense to talk about things that happened **in the past / in the present.**

In 1950, the boys **used to** wear shorts.
They **didn't use to** have computers.
Did you **use to** have lunch at school when you were young?
Yes, we **did.** / No, we **didn't.**

Circle the correct option.
We use **used to / going to** to talk about things we did in the past, but don't do now.

Think Again!

What's the difference between these groups of verbs in the past tense?

bring	play
write	look
be	work
sit	study

Dialogue Maker: Talk to a friend about school in the past.

Did they	wear	uniforms?
	use	pants?
		computers?
		hula-hoops?
Yes, they did. / No, they didn't.		

Did the boys and girls	have to	sit separately?
		use laptops in class?

Did they use to	use	laptops?
		encyclopedias?
		download music?
		chat online?
	have	TVs?
		pizza for lunch?

Chapter 2 Grammar

I**'ve lived** here for 35 years.
He**'s lived** here for three years.
How long **have** you **lived** in Japan?
I**'ve lived** here **for** three years / **since** I was five.

Circle the correct option.
We use the **present progressive / present perfect** tense to talk about something that began in the past and continues now.

I**'m going to** go to music school.
She **isn't going to** go to college.
He **might** be a singer.
What **are** you **going to** do?
Are you **going to** be a doctor?

Circle the correct option.
We use **might / going to** to talk about things we've decided to do in the future.

Think Again!

What's the difference between *I'm going to be a dentist* and *I might be a dentist?*

Dialogue Maker: **Talk to a friend about your plans.**

What are you going to do?		
I'm going to / I might	go	to college.
		to Europe.
	work	in a hospital.
		very hard.
	be	famous.
		a dentist.
Are you going to	travel?	
	study?	
	be a doctor?	
Yes, I am / No, I'm not. / I don't know. I might …		

Chapter 3 Grammar

Think Again!
What's the comparative form of *good* and *bad*?

The movie **isn't as** good **as** the book. = The book is **better than** the movie.
The book **wasn't as** interesting **as** the movie. = The movie was **more interesting than** the book.
The book was **just as** good **as** the movie. = The movie was **just as** good **as** the book.

Circle the correct option.
The comparative form of **long** / **short** words is *more* (+ adjective) *than*.
We can also use *not as* (adjective) *as* to make comparisons.

The book is boring. I feel **bored.**
I'm disappointed. The movie was **disappointing.**

Circle the correct option.
The ***-ing*** / ***-ed*** adjective tells you how somebody feels.

Dialogue Maker: **Talk to a friend. Compare a book and a movie.**

What do you think of the book/movie?		
I think the book/movie is	better	than the movie/book.
	more frightening	

It's	not as	good	as …
		bad	
	just as	realistic	

I was	bored.
	disappointed.
	confused.

I thought it was	awful.
	amazing.

Grammar Reference

Chapter 4 Grammar

We**'re** fly**ing** to New York tomorrow.
I**'m not** go**ing** to school.
Are you eat**ing** at Joe's Café on Tuesday?

Circle the correct option.
We use the present progressive to talk about things we **have arranged to do / might do** in the future.

Someone gave me a book.
I'd like to do **something** exciting.
I don't know **anything** about the Montgolfier brothers.
Did **anyone** travel in it?
No one wants to visit the café today.

Circle the correct option.
We usually use *something* or *someone* in **positive / negative** sentences and *anything* or *anyone* in **positive / negative** sentences and questions. *No one* or *nothing* is used in **positive / negative** sentences.

Think Again!

What's the difference between *There was someone in the room* and *There was something in the room?*

Dialogue Maker: **Talk to a friend about your plans.**

What are you doing	on Thursday?
	for vacation?

I'm	traveling to America.
	visiting a friend.

Are you going by	plane?
	car?
I'm going by ...	

Is anyone going with you?	
Yes, someone	is going with me.
No, no one	

Chapter 5 Grammar

What**'s** the bag **made of**? It**'s made of** cotton.
What**'s** the bag **used for**?
It**'s used for** carrying shopping.

Circle the correct option.
We use the passive *is made of* and *is used for* because we **are / are not** interested in the person who made the bag or who carries the shopping.

Soccer **is played** at my school.
English **is spoken** in lots of countries.

Circle the correct option.
Is played and *is spoken* are passive.
We use the **active / passive** when we're more interested in what's happening than the person doing it.

Think Again!

How do we make the passive? Which verb forms do we use?

Dialogue Maker: **Ask a friend some quiz questions.**

Where's	Spanish spoken?		Spanish is spoken	in	Spain / Mexico / India / China.
	cotton grown?		Cotton is grown		

What's	glass	made of?	Glass	is made of	sand / cocoa.
	chocolate		Chocolate		

Where are	pandas found?	Pandas are found	in	China / Thailand.
	elephants ridden?	Elephants are ridden		

Chapter 6 Grammar

I **was** do**ing** my homework when you **walked** in.
We **were** watch**ing** TV when the doorbell **rang**.

Circle the correct option.
We use **was** / **is** + verb + *-ing* to make the past progressive tense.

While you **were reading** the story, I **fell** asleep.
When I **fell** asleep, you **were reading** the story.
What **were** you **doing when** the ship **sank**?

Circle the correct option.
We often use **while** / **when** before the past progressive tense and **while** / **when** before the simple past tense.

Think Again!
What's the difference between the past progressive and the simple past tense?

Dialogue Maker: **Talk to a friend about what they were doing yesterday at a specific time.**

What	were you	doing at	6 o'clock	yesterday evening?
	was your mom		10 o'clock	last night?

I was	eating dinner.
	watching TV.
She was	doing homework.
	sleeping.

What happened while	she was	sleeping?
	you were	eating dinner?

My	dad	walked in.
	friend	called me.

I	fell asleep.
	heard a loud noise.

Grammar Reference

Chapter 7 Grammar

That's very noisy. Can you do that **quietly**, please?
I did very **badly** on the exam. I couldn't answer anything.

Circle the correct option.
Adverbs tell us how somebody does something. They tell us more about a verb.
Many adverbs are made by adding ***-ly* / *-er*** to an adjective.

I eat **too many** cookies and I drink **too much** cola.
I don't drink **enough** water and I don't eat **enough** vegetables.

Circle the correct option.
Too much and *too many* are the opposite of *not enough*. We use *too much* with **uncountable / countable** nouns (e.g. *salt, sugar*) and *too many* with **countable / uncountable** nouns (e.g. *apples, potato chips*).

Think Again!

Do we put *too many*, *too much*, and *not enough* before or after the noun in a sentence?

Dialogue Maker: Talk to a friend about eating habits.

Do you	eat	enough	vegetables / fruit	every day?
	drink		water / juice	

Yes, I do.	I eat …
No, I don't.	I drink …

Do you	eat	too much	chocolate / sugar / salt / fat?	
		too many	candy bars / potato chips?	
	drink	too many	cans of / glasses of	soda?
		too much		coffee?

Yes, I do.	I eat …
No, I don't.	I drink …

Chapter 8 Grammar

"I'**m** very happy." She said (that) she **was** very happy.
"I **don't like** traveling." She explained (that) she **didn't like** traveling.

Circle the correct option.
In reported speech, the present form in direct speech changes to the **past / future** form.

"Where **do you live**?" He asked where **I lived**.
"**Do you like** reading?" She asked **if I liked** reading.

Circle the correct option.
In reported questions, the present form usually changes to the past form and the word order **changes / doesn't change.**

Think Again!

When do we use *if* in reported questions?

Dialogue Maker: **Talk to a friend about a phone call you had.**

I spoke to my	dad	yesterday.
	grandma	last weekend.
	friend	

What did	he	say?
	she	

He / She	told me	(that)…	
	said		
	asked me	if	I was well.
		what	I wanted for my birthday.
		when	I could come and visit.

What did you say?				
I	said	(that)	I was	well.
	explained			
	told her		I wanted a new bike.	
			I could come and visit next weekend.	

Chapter 9 Grammar

In the future, …
everyone **will travel** by bike or tram.
you **won't need** a car.

Circle the correct option.
After *will* and *won't,* we use the verb (e.g. *live, be able to, learn, go, travel*) **with / without** *to.*

Will we **drive** cars? Yes, we **will**. / No, we **won't**.
What **will** people **wear**?

Circle the correct option.
We can begin questions about the **future / present** with *will* or a question word (*what, when, how,* etc.).

Think Again!
What is the contracted form of *will not?*

Dialogue Maker: **Talk to a friend about the future.**

What will	houses	be like in the future?
	schools	
	clothes	

How will we travel?			
We	will	use	
	won't		driverless cars.
			flying cars.

What will we have at home?			
We	will	have	wind turbines.
	won't		touch screen controls.

People	will	live	under the ground.
			on Mars.
		study	at home.
	won't		with robots.
		wear	gadgets.
			strange clothes.

Macmillan Education
4 Crinan Street
London N1 9XW
A division of Macmillan Publishers Limited

Companies and representatives throughout the world

ISBN 978-0-230-45232-9
Pack ISBN 978-0-230-45233-6

First published 2015

Designed by Wild Apple Design Ltd
Illustrated by Alberto Arzeni (Advocate Art) pp30–31, 32; Pedro Bascon (Advocate Art) pp50–51, 52: Sanjay Charlton (Beehive Illustration) pp20–21, 22, 24; Pablo Gallego (Beehive Illustration) pp18, 34, 74, 77; Roy Knipe (Good Illustration) pp60–61, 62, 64; Fabio Leone pp80–81, 82, 84; Mike Love (Bright Agency) pp10-11, 12, 14; Paul McCaffery (Sylvie Poggio Artist Agency) pp90–91, 92; Laszlo Veres (Beehive Illustration) pp8, 27, 37, 38, 45, 47, 68, 88, 97; Steven Wood (Advocate Art) pp4–104 (border design and main character artwork) 4–5, 6–7, 10, 13, 20, 23, 30, 33, 40, 43, 50, 53, 60, 63, 70, 73, 80, 83, 90, 93.
Cover design by Wild Apple Design Ltd
Cover artwork by Steven Wood (Advocate Art)
Cover photographs by Paul Bricknell
Picture research by Victoria Gaunt

Authors' acknowledgements
Thank you to everyone at Macmillan for their support and for allowing us to work in 'our way'. For patience and tolerance of late-night working, thank you to our families.

The authors and publishers would like to thank the following for permission to reproduce their photographs:
Alamy/Bon Appetit p54(bl), Alamy/Richard Cooper p49(tr), Alamy/Derek Croucher p54(cl), Alamy/Alistair Heap p49(br), Alamy/Hemis p39(cr),Alamy/D Hurst p39(cr), Alamy/imagebroke p94(tml), Alamy/adam james p75(l), Alamy/Oleg p57(tm), Alamy/Trevor Pearson p69(t), Alamy/philipus p57(tl, tr), Alamy/Simon Rawles p54(tl), Alamy/Philip Scalia p87, Alamy/ Neil Setchfield p75(r), Alamy/StockPhotosArt p39(br); **BrandX** p94(tmr); **The Bridgeman Art Library**/Sterling & Francine Clark Art Institute, Williamstown, Massachusetts, USA p55(br); **Corbis** pp9(r), 65, Corbis/Bettman p15(r), Corbis/ClassicStock p17, Corbis/Michael Cole p15(l), Corbis/Macduff Everton p54(background), Corbis/Franck Guiziou/Hemis p55(tr, background), Corbis/ENZO RUSSO/epa p59, Corbis/Leser/SoFood p54(tr); **Getty Images** 18(br), 58(r), Getty Images/AFP p54(br), Getty Images/Doug Allan p58(background), Getty Images/Oliver Lopez Asis p39(tl), Getty Images/Matt Brasier p94(tr), Getty Images/Niels Busch p28(tl), Getty Images/Echo p28(bm), Getty Images/Steve Granitz p86(Adele), Getty Images/U.S. Coast Guard/digital version by Science Faction p58(l), Getty Images/M Gungen Photography p67, Getty Images/Wendy Idele p78(t),Getty Images/Dave & Les Jacobs p28(tm), Getty Images/Rob Lewine p28(bl), Getty Images/kali9 p79, Getty Images/Thapakorn Karnosod p19(l), Getty Images/Mike Kemp pp18(tl), 28(tr), Getty Images/Julian Love p49(bm), Getty Images/Laurence Monneret p39(tr), Getty Images/paul mansfield photography p18(tm), Getty Images/Sean Murphy p28(br), Getty Images/Patrick Sheandell O'Carroll p48(1), Getty Images/Ariel Skelley p78(c),Getty Images/SPARKLAR p48(2), Getty Images/Nicholas Rigg p35(t), Getty Images/Image Source pp94(bl, tm), Getty Images/Chris Stein p19(r), Getty Images/Muammer Mujdat Uzel p35(b); **Macmillan Publishers Ltd** pp29, 48(4), 94(tl), Macmillan Publishers Ltd/Paul Bricknell p94(br); **Raleigh International** pp25(t,b,c); **REX**/PASCAL VILA/V.S.D./SIPA pp95(br,t,bl), REX/Isopix p95(bm); **Superstock**/Flirt p45; **Thinkstock** p48(3), Thinkstock/Mile Atanasov p48(6), Thinkstock/Franck Boston p28(boy), Thinkstock/Jose manuel Gelpi diaz p9(l), Thinkstock/LanaDjuric/istock p57(b), Thinkstock/JosT Elias p35(tc), Thinkstock/Liesel Fuchs p18(bl), Thinkstock/Fuse p78(b), Thinkstock/Meliha Gojak p48(5), Thinkstock/ivansmuk p49(bl), Thinkstock/lalouetto p48(7), Thinkstock/nickname p39(br), Thinkstock/PaulPaladin p35(bc), Thinkstock/pederk p55(tm), Thinkstock/joshuaraineyphotography p54(cr), Thinkstock/Sdenisov p49(tl), Thinkstock/SeanPavonePhoto p39(bm), Thinkstock/Digital Vision. P18(tr).
Commissioned photographs by MMStudios pp16, 26, 36, 46, 56, 66, 76, 86, 96.
Prop Artwork by Carla Drury

We would like to thank the following for their help with the photos in the book: Henry, Hollie, Rocco and Sofia.

Printed and bound in Thailand

2019 2018 2017 2016
10 9 8 7 6 5 4